Inspiring Curiosity

A Librarian's Guide to Inquiry-Based Learning

Colette Cassinelli

International Society for Technology in Education
PORTLAND, OREGON • ARLINGTON, VIRGINIA

Inspiring Curiosity
A Librarian's Guide to Inquiry-Based Learning
Colette Cassinelli

© 2018 International Society for Technology in Education
World rights reserved. No part of this book may be reproduced or transmitted in any form or by any means—electronic, mechanical, photocopying, recording, or by any information storage or retrieval system—without prior written permission from the publisher. Contact Permissions Editor: iste.org/about/permissions-and-reprints; permissions@iste.org; fax: 1.541.302.3780.

Acquisitions Editor: *Valerie Witte*
Editor: *Emily Reed*
Copy Editor: *Karstin Painter*
Proofreader: *Corinne Gould*
Book Design and Production: *Kim McGovern*
Cover Design: *Edwin Ouellette*

Library of Congress Cataloging-in-Publication Data available

First Edition
ISBN: 978-1-56484-672-3
Ebook version available.

Printed in the United States of America

ISTE® is a registered trademark of the International Society for Technology in Education.

About ISTE

The International Society for Technology in Education (ISTE) is the premier nonprofit organization serving educators and education leaders committed to empowering connected learners in a connected world. ISTE serves more than 100,000 education stakeholders throughout the world.

ISTE's innovative offerings include the ISTE Conference & Expo, one of the biggest, most comprehensive ed tech events in the world—as well as the widely adopted ISTE Standards for learning, teaching and leading in the digital age and a robust suite of professional learning resources, including webinars, online courses, consulting services for schools and districts, books, and peer-reviewed journals and publications. Visit iste.org to learn more.

Related ISTE Titles

Digital Age Librarians Series

Reimagining Library Spaces: Transform Your Space on Any Budget by Diana Rendina

    This practical guide shares tips for affordably transforming library spaces, how-tos for hosting makerspaces and learning labs, and suggestions for supporting BYOD.

Connected Librarians: Tap Social Media to Enhance Professional Development and Student Learning by Nikki D Robertson

    This engaging book provides the professional development librarians need to understand how to use social media effectively to improve student learning.

To see all books available from ISTE, please visit iste.org/resources.

About the Author

Colette Cassinelli is a library instructional technology teacher at Sunset High School in Beaverton, Oregon, with over twenty-five years of teaching experience in grades K–16. With a master's degree in Educational Technology and from Pepperdine University in Library/Media from Portland State, she is as a lifelong learner who is always on the lookout for great information literacy or technology integration lessons to share with faculty. Cassinelli is a Google Certified Innovator and has presented at local and national library and technology conferences including the Northwest Council for Computer Education (NCCE), the ISTE Conference & Expo, EdTechTeam Google Summits, and the Oregon Association of School Libraries (OASL).

Acknowledgments

Thanks to fellow teachers and staff at Sunset High School in Beaverton, Oregon. You always say, "Yes" and strive for innovation. Thanks especially to Chris Bick, Rebecca Larson, Tara Slaughter, Alisa Harvey, Andrew Brown, Paul Hampton, Stephanie Lalley, Lindsey Mockel, and Matt Hiefield for sharing their stories.

I have met so many wonderful people through Twitter, by reading blogs, and face-to-face at librarian and EdTech conferences. It's wonderful to hear about the good work you do in your schools and communities. Thanks especially to librarians Rosa Rothenberger, Michelle Luhtala, Carolyn Foote, Tiffany Whitehead, Stony Evans, Tasha Bergson-Michelson, Nikki

Robertson, Shannon Miller, and many more. I love reading educator blogs and publications, and appreciate those who shared their own learning and reflection.

A special thank you to Suzie Boss and Leslie Maniotes for sharing their expertise. I am truly inspired by your work.

Finally, thanks to my husband, Dave, and my family who cheered and encouraged me throughout this process. You have always been behind me as I take new risks and challenges.

Dedication

I dedicate this book to Alan and Matthew.

> The future belongs to those who believe in the beauty of their dreams.
> —ELEANOR ROOSEVELT

Contents

Foreword xi

Introduction 1

CHAPTER 1
Creating A Schoolwide Culture of Inquiry 5
    Inquiry-Based Learning 7
    Librarian's Role 8
    Digital Age Pedagogy 9
    National School Library Standards 11
    Culture of Empowerment 13
    Culture of Risk Taking 13
    Culture of Sharing 14
    Culture of Openness 15
    Culture of Literacy 17
    Our Task 19

CHAPTER 2
Librarian's Role with Inquiry-Based Learning 21
    Developing Collaborative Partnerships 22
    Build Relationships 23
    Be of Value 23
    Show Empathy 24
    Get Involved 24
    Types of Inquiry 26
    Curriculum Planning 30

CHAPTER 3
Inspiring Curiosity 39
    Curiosity Comes First 40
    Librarian's Role 40
    Powerful Openers 42
    Problem-Based Learning 54
    Design Thinking 56

Project-Based Learning 58
Geography Tools 61

CHAPTER 4
Developing Effective Questions 65
Question Formulation Technique 66
Students Ask the Questions 68
Develop a Culture of Thinking Using Visible Thinking 69
Genius Hour 71
Librarian's Role 72
Mentor Groups 74

CHAPTER 5
Diving Into The Research Process 77
Imagine the Perfect Source 78
Teaching Search 80
Curating Sources 83
Helpful Hints 84
Student Curation Tools 86
Developing a Researcher's Mindset 88
Credibility Source Investigators 90
Interrogate Your Source 91
Plagiarism 92
Note-Taking Strategies 94
Google Forms 97
Ebooks for Beginner Researchers 98
Differentiation 100
Sentence Frames 101
Paragraph Summary with Source Integration 103

CHAPTER 6
Publishing and Performance Tasks 108
Authentic Audience 109
Online Communities 111
Publishing Options 112
Standards 114

Inspiring Stories of Publishing and Sharing........................... 116

CHAPTER 7
Assessment and Inquiry Tools....................................... 122
Formative Assessment 124
Peer and Self-Assessment.. 128
Inquiry Circle 129
Rubrics 130
Summative Assessments 133
Performance Tasks... 135
Librarian's Role 135

CHAPTER 8
Reflection for Deeper Learning....................................... 139
Reflecting on Content and Process....................................... 140
Benefits of Reflection.. 141
Reflection Techniques.. 142
Reflection Questions 143
Librarian Involvement with Reflection................................... 144
Reflective Practices for the Inquiry Teachers........................... 145

CHAPTER 9
Librarian's Call to Action.. 148
Get Started on Your Journey!.. 149

References 153

APPENDIX A
ISTE Standards 159
ISTE Standards for Students.. 159

APPENDIX B
Recommended Reading... 163

APPENDIX C
Discussion Questions 164

Foreword

When the Beaverton School District finally decided to reinstate librarians after years of dramatic budget cuts, the position evolved into something brand new: The "Library Instructional Technology Teacher" would now be called upon to both direct the library and guide a 1:1 digital initiative that included providing Chromebooks to every one of our high school students.

At Sunset High School these daunting responsibilities included reframing the teaching and learning experience for 2,200+ students and providing differentiated professional development for 120 licensed staff members. The skills demanded by this job called for a teacher of incomparable knowledge, talent, and drive. Colette Cassinelli quickly proved to be exactly the right person for this role.

A master teacher with over twenty-five years of K–16 experience, Colette made an immediate and indelible impact on our school community with her visionary thinking and leadership. Never one to be satisfied with the status quo, Colette reshaped our daily experiences by coaching teachers on how to infuse technology into their classrooms and by helping students maximize their potential through the design of contemporary and relevant learning experiences.

Inspiring Curiosity: A Librarian's Guide to Inquiry-Based Learning is an outgrowth of Colette's collaborative, inquiry-first approach to education. The stories and research that are shared here are powerful testimonials to what is possible when we "empower students to take risks and allow their questions and curiosity to take center stage." It is a book for anyone who believes that there is no higher calling than helping students take charge of their own learning.

Chris Bick
Vice Principal
Sunset High School

Introduction

Too often secondary instruction is full of: science lab reports where the questions and conclusions contain the same information, 125 essays written by different students on the same historical topic, book reviews where summaries are plagiarized and passed off as original, PowerPoint slides filled with text that is "PowerPointless," and so on.

This is not learning—this is following a recipe. Students in today's schools trudge through assignments that aren't personally meaningful in the name of mastering a certain number of learning targets and "covering material." Learning in a vacuum without relevance and personal interests falls short. Yes, our high school students can compose a formulated five-paragraph essay, but can they defend and argue on topics that are truly meaningful and have an impact on their lives?

In this book, *Inspiring Curiosity: A Librarian's Guide to Inquiry-Based Learning*, I hope to challenge librarians and classroom teachers to not only re-evaluate their goals, techniques, and procedures for teaching research—but to transform it. Sir Ken Robinson stated in his book *The Element: How Finding Your Passion Changes Everything* (2009),

> The fact is that given the challenges we face, education doesn't need to be reformed—it needs to be transformed. The key to this transformation is not to standardize education, but to personalize it, to build achievement on discovering the individual talents of each child, to put students in an environment where they want to learn and where they can naturally discover their true passions.

Introduction

In my thirty plus years as an educator teaching every grade level from K–16, I have witnessed first-hand students who are transformed and engaged in meaningful work. I have empathized with students so consumed and frustrated with immigration issues that they cry out, "I thought I understood the issues, but now I don't know!" I remember a student begging his history teacher for more time during their Socratic seminar because he "needed" to share with his classmates what he learned and wanted to influence their thinking. I've helped students track down information in hard-to-find college databases because they were passionate about their topic and wanted to learn more.

These moments have encouraged me to keep passion and inquiry at the center of my students' experience and the focus of my instruction. I constantly strive to find relevant topics that pique student interest or provide opportunities to do work that matters. I have hit road blocks of curriculum pacing and administrative directives, but have always strived to give my students authentic reasons to publish and share their work with an audience who cares.

Inquiry-based learning puts the student in the driver's seat and allows them to steer the direction of their learning. Our job as educators—whether you are an administrator, librarian, classroom teacher, or support staff—is to create an environment where this can thrive. We need to move away from compartmentalized knowledge towards multidisciplinary collaborative learning. We need to reframe what we are asking secondary students to do in school and empower them to take risks and apply what they know in real-world contexts. I hope this book inspires you to do the same.

Chapter 1 lays the foundation of inquiry-based learning and the pedagogical shift required for student agency. It asks you to review the culture of your school and evaluate whether students and teachers are empowered, take risks, work collaboratively together, celebrate learning, and value literacy. Reviewing the ISTE Standards for Students (2016) and the National School Library Standards allows you to align your work and make goals for the future.

Chapter 2 challenges school librarians to build a strong foundation with their staff so they can work collaboratively and truly impact student learning. We look at various levels of inquiry (confirmation, structured, guided, or open inquiry) and discuss matching the instructional goals to the lesson. Suggestions for structuring inquiry lessons using Understanding by Design or Guided Inquiry Design are explored.

An extensive resource list of powerful openers for inquiry lessons are provided in Chapter 3. Oftentimes classroom teachers need new ideas to spark curiosity and engage students in meaningful conversations before they begin a personalized inquiry project. Activities around social justice issues, films, current events, or discussions with experts can engage students and provide context for their research. Problem-based learning, design thinking, and project-based learning provide insight and inspiration for structured inquiry lessons.

Chapter 4 explores how student generated questions are at the heart of inquiry-based learning. Readers will learn about the Question Formulation Technique and Visible Thinking routines as ways of helping students to fine-tune their thinking and invest themselves in quality work that matters.

Chapter 5 dives deep into the research process with ideas like "imagining the perfect source" and teaching students how to effectively search. Ideas are given for curating sources, developing a researcher's mindset, and evaluating sources for authority and credibility. Note-taking strategies and ideas for differentiation are shared to make the learning experience personalized.

Introduction

Publishing and performance tasks are discussed in Chapter 6. Stories of how students research and shared their learning with real audiences are highlighted, as well as technology tools for publishing.

Chapter 7 and 8 provide ideas for assessment and explains how to use inquiry tools throughout the research process. The benefits of reflection are explored as well as ideas of how the librarian can be more involved in assessment and reflection activities.

Finally, Chapter 9 is a librarian's call to action. Instead of being relegated to the beginning of the research instruction, librarians are encouraged to be involved in all aspects of inquiry-based learning.

Thank you for selecting this book, and I hope it opens your eyes to new possibilities and inspires you to share what you learn with your colleagues.

CHAPTER 1

Creating A Schoolwide Culture of Inquiry

One afternoon in the school library, I had a casual conversation with one of my students that led her down an interesting line of inquiry. Kate, a senior in the IB history class at Sunset High School, was talking about her upcoming Internal Assessment (a historical assessment). Kate was considering the topic of occupied France during WWII for her senior history research project. She had developed an interest in the topic during her junior year, after reading the novel *All The Light We Cannot See* by Anthony Doerr. She was doing some background reading to get a sense of the issues during the time period.

CHAPTER 1 | Creating A Schoolwide Culture of Inquiry

I shared that my own father had been a teenager during WWII, and his family had been evicted from their home in Vire, France, in 1943. Their home had been occupied by the German army for two years, so the family moved in with my father's grandmother. One can imagine the turmoil.

Kate was genuinely interested, so I also shared that my uncle still had a journal of his experiences that he had written in secondary school. We discussed how smart it was of my uncle's forward-thinking teacher to ask students to reflect on their experiences. Eventually, I asked Kate if she would she be interested in a video recording of my uncle reading from his journal and reminiscing with my father about growing up in the Normandy region. Kate said yes, so I sent her the YouTube video and directed her to print and online sources from our school library to get her started.

Kate's history teacher encouraged the class to take advantage of the local public library to locate academic journals and primary source documents using the JSTOR database. Kate visited Multnomah County Library and worked with a librarian there to reserve some titles. After some initial research, she was leaning toward the idea of how French identity changed during the occupation. "All of my background research has made me more confused, and I am trying to work out those ideas. It's still kind of murky," she reported after a week.

Kate experienced the natural uncertainty that occurs when a student has some solid research but hasn't adequately narrowed a research question. I encouraged Kate to look at sources outside of the American view of the war and see if she could find stories or speeches from the French resistance, perhaps newspapers or artifacts from a French museum, or the World Digital Library. Exploring the psychology of how culture is formed and how people under siege maintain a sense of self piqued her interest, and Kate produced even more questions and ideas. She was well on her way to becoming a curious researcher.

Inquiry-Based Learning

Kate's story illustrates the transformational experience of a student personally engaged in authentic inquiry-based learning. Curiosity fuels students' passion to make connections with topics that are meaningful and real. By engaging in deep thinking and asking thought-provoking questions, students are challenged to consider new perspectives. Kate was offered plenty of choice and autonomy in selecting her topic, but it was her personal interest that made the difference. A hallmark of inquiry-based learning is that students' own driving questions propel their research. That spark of curiosity bridges the gap between what they know and do not know. Learners steer the direction of their inquiry as they consider the best way to uncover stories or unexpected ideas. Compare Kate's situation to the chorus of groans when a teacher assigns everyone to investigate a specific topic. Provocative and open-ended inquiry asks students to respond and think critically. As the research progresses, students organize and unpack information to assimilate new concepts. Notice how Kate leveraged the resources of her public library to gain additional sources beyond her school library. Using inquiry-based learning, students conduct interviews, formulate opinions, defend stances, or develop creative solutions connected to their original questions. Students are provided opportunities to present what they learned through writing or multimedia channels. Students may feel compelled to take action or extend their research to the community. Finally, inquiry-based learners reflect on what they have learned and accomplished. I was thrilled that my family history resonated with Kate and helped move her research forward. Inquiry-based learning is more than a research paper or asking questions at the beginning of a unit. It requires students to take on the researcher's mindset and internalize concepts for themselves. Who knows? Long after her assignment is complete, this inquiry project may kindle Kate's desire to know even more about life during WWII.

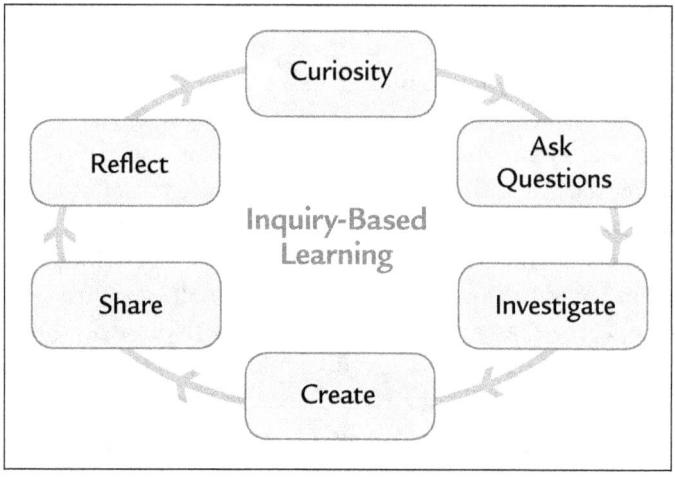

Figure 1.1 Elements of Inquiry-Based Learning.

Librarian's Role

What is the school librarian's role throughout the inquiry-based learning experience? How can we impact the learning experience for our students and make a difference? I will provide inspiring stories and practical examples of how school librarians can become essential members of an instructional team by moving beyond the basics of teaching students how to access and evaluate sources.

Not every inquiry-based lesson will develop into an in-depth research project or essay. Many will result in engaging Socratic seminars where students debate and explore ideas with their classmates. Other inquiry-based lessons might lead students to investigate science phenomena or the creation of "wonder walls" to document new questions of inquiry. I am interested in finding those key entry points where librarians can insert themselves into inquiry-based lessons and offer expertise and insights unique to our positions. Librarians can do more than just guide learners toward digital and print sources. We work directly with every student and every teacher in our school. We see the bigger picture and can view the landscape of our school through the lens of inquiry. We can influence the tone and direction of how students see themselves as researchers. In collaboration with your administration and faculty, examine your school's curriculum and identify entry points where you can play a crucial role in shaping secondary students to be career and college ready. Not every experience will have a personal connection like Kate had with me, but every librarian can focus on personalized learning and ensure we are preparing teens for their future.

Digital Age Pedagogy

Our challenge as educators is to propel the pedagogical shift forward, toward a culture of innovation and creativity. Traditional approaches that emphasize memorization or "looking up" facts do not strengthen critical thinking skills. It is no longer acceptable to have students recall names, dates, and figures when many teens have access to this digital content at their fingertips. The world has changed, and every major institution is quickly evolving. Chris Bick, Vice Principal at Sunset High School, reflects, "No one benefits from the nostalgic view of their own childhood education. We will not be preparing kids for the world that they are destined to inherit if we continue to stand still." (C. Bick, personal communication, November 16, 2017) A culture of innovation—a way of doing things new and better—needs to pervade every single lesson. Bick suggests

> **21st Century Pedagogy**
>
> - Inquiry-Based
> - Relevant
> - Authentic
> - Active
> - Collaborative
> - Reflective

Figure 1.2 21st Century Pedagogy.

librarians work intentionally with their faculty in moving this dial forward. When librarians collaborate with classroom teachers, they can be "that innovative thinker that makes sure a picture of that future is painted with great clarity." (2017)

Inquiry-based strategies are a significant facet of a twent first century pedagogy (see Figure 1.2). Giving students agency (control over what they experience) changes their self-image from passive receivers of information to leaders who are invested in their own learning. Student's questions and intense curiosity drive learning forward. Authentic inquiry will not only engage students but develop higher-order skills and present them with opportunities to communicate effectively to a wide range of audiences. All students need to feel empowered and to know they can make a difference. Inquiry-based projects that ask students how they can serve others will build empathy and compassion.

Tony Wagner, Ed.D., Expert in Residence at Harvard University's Innovation Lab states,

> The capacity to innovate—to solve problems creatively or to bring new possibilities to life—is the single most important competitive advantage for individuals and organizations. In today's world, it is not what you know—it's what you can do with what you know. (2012b)

Wagner has identified seven survival skills for success (2017), as defined by business leaders:

1. Critical thinking and problem solving
2. Collaboration across networks and leading by influence
3. Agility and adaptability
4. Initiative and entrepreneurship
5. Effective oral and written communication
6. Accessing and analyzing information
7. Curiosity and imagination

To reshape education toward a culture of innovation, we need to move away from compartmentalized knowledge toward collaboration and sustained opportunities for multidisciplinary problem solving. How do we shift our secondary students from compliance to engagement to empowerment? Inquiry-based learning demands that students ask hard questions and embrace uncertainty. How do we create a culture of risk taking that fosters intrinsic motivation among our teens? Schools with a culture of innovation "teach students to view trial and error—and failure—as integral to the problem-solving process." Do we provide opportunities to create and use their knowledge in applied contexts? These are all excellent questions that lead us to evaluate the culture of inquiry schoolwide (Wagner, 2012a).

National School Library Standards

The American Association of School Librarians (AASL) identifies beliefs central to our profession in the *National School Library Standards for Learners, School Librarians, and School Libraries* (2018b).

1. The school library is a unique and essential part of a learning community.
2. Qualified school librarians lead effective school libraries.
3. Learners should be prepared for college, career, and life.
4. Reading is the core of personal and academic competency.
5. Intellectual freedom is every learner's right.
6. Information technologies must be appropriately integrated and equitably available.

Our leadership as school librarians provides access to high-quality resources and connects classroom instruction to real-world events. We develop and direct information literacy lessons and help to integrate technology throughout the curriculum. We entice readers by selecting and promoting high-quality reading material. Self-directed learning in the library is the central core of personalized learning. Our libraries help foster students' personal interests, and they encourage students to become life-long learners. Librarians champion the rights of all readers and make sure everyone has equitable access to print and digital resources. Review the AASL *National Library Standards for Learners* that are framed around the shared foundations (Inquire, Include, Collaborate, Curate, Explore, and Engage) and embrace progressive pedagogies. Our challenge is to create a learning culture centered on innovation, collaboration, exploration, deep thinking, and creativity. The AASL *National Library Standards for Learners* (2018) encourages librarians to embrace progressive pedagogies:

> School librarians are key to the success of this educational paradigm shift because they provide resources and instruction to all learners through an inquiry-based research model that supports questioning and the creation of new knowledge focused on learner interest and real-world problems. (44)

Culture of Empowerment

Creating a schoolwide culture that values inquiry and empowerment doesn't just happen automatically; it begins with the administration and can take various forms. Is there a clear public statement of beliefs and norms that is actively used during faculty meetings? Having shared decision-making protocols in place can facilitate this schoolwide culture. It sends a powerful message when we empower all educators to work together to establish a culture where everyone's voice is considered (Guide to Collaborative Culture and Shared Leadership, 2001). School administrators can create policies that support flexible learning teams so they have time to share resources and design, implement, and reflect together on inquiry-based lessons. Regularly scheduled periods for collaboration across departments are essential for quality instructional units. It is unfeasible for the librarian to attend grade-level meetings or be involved in evaluating the effectiveness of unit plans without this scheduled time. It is almost impossible to be innovative on your own.

Culture of Risk Taking

If our goal is to create schools where secondary students feel safe to take risks, sometimes fail, and bounce back with resiliency, then we need to do the same with teachers and librarians. If schools want teachers to shift toward inquiry-based learning, then there needs to be a level of trust and empowerment within the organization. A. J. Juliani, author of *Inquiry and Innovation in the Classroom: Using 20% time, Genius Hour, and PBL to Drive Student Success*, suggests school leaders offer new ways of measuring, praising, and assessing teachers based on creative and innovative pursuits. Juliani blogs about building a culture of innovation at your school and shares a quote from Tim Brown,

CEO of Ideo, who offers advice on building a culture of innovation: "If people get penalized for failure, particularly the kind of failure that's most useful which is where you learn a lot, then they're not going to do it, in which case you're not going to get any innovation" (as cited in Juliani, 2017). We want educators to embrace a growth mindset and have some autonomy and choice in their professional learning decisions.

Culture of Sharing

What your school celebrates says a lot about what you value as a community. Is learning celebrated at your school? Deep learning can be recognized at the classroom level, in the library, or through schoolwide events like science fairs, innovation celebrations, and community-outreach events. I love this quote in Figure 1.3 from sixth-grade teacher Bill Ferriter, who shares that genuine learning is a joyful act worthy of celebration (2015). Each year the students at your school should proudly proclaim,

> "I am in the ____ grade at _____ school, and this year we get to study _____."

Do teachers have "signature projects" that students look forward to every year? Building a compelling schoolwide brand distinguishes your academic program.

Are you on the school leadership team? Meeting regularly with the administration or professional development team not only involves you in essential school decisions but also sends a strong message to the faculty that your work is valued and necessary. If you don't meet regularly with administrators, add this as your professional goal for next year and explain the value you can offer. Consider sending quarterly reports to your administrative staff showcasing your work, and include data to back up your impact.

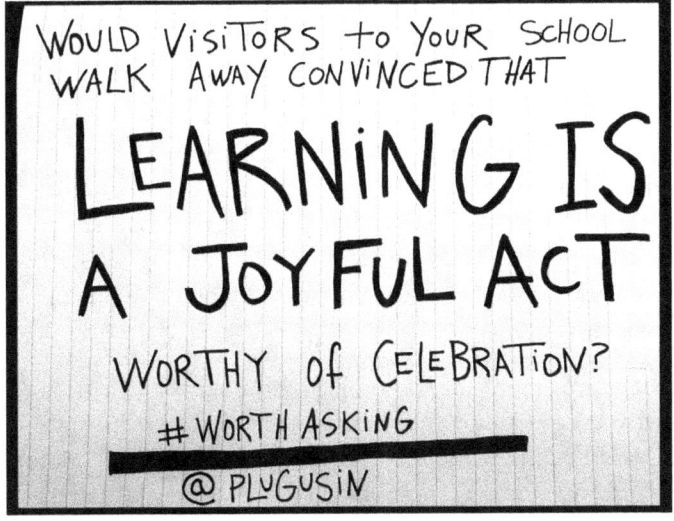

Figure 1.3 Learning is a Genuine Act.

Culture of Openness

Teachers and librarians are guides who cultivate wonder and challenge students to think as historians, scientists, writers, and artists. Our students consider diverse concepts as they take risks in forming opinions or debating ideas. Are there opportunities for your students to discuss and refine thinking? Are all questions and ideas thoughtfully considered, or are they pushed aside because we need to move on and "cover" the curriculum. Critical thinking takes shape as students collaboratively build understanding through inquiry circles, within Socratic seminars, or during reflection. It takes time, patience, and a shift in teaching strategies to design an inquiry classroom where ideas can flourish. Science teacher Ramsey Musallam embraces openness to improve his craft of teaching. How does he do it? Each quarter, Musallam spends his prep time working in the back of a colleague's classroom. He explains, "I cannot overemphasize how incredibly impactful and simple this process has been. Each day I leave my prep period with my lessons planned and an invaluable list of strategies I want to try" (2015, p.88). If you try this, not only will you have an awareness of the student experience, you will see your fellow teachers in a new light. Are you using peer observations to make your library or classroom a place where students take an active role in learning? We can learn strategies and new approaches when embrace an open door policy.

ISTE Standards for Students emphasize the skills and attributes we want our students to embrace in our connected and digital world. Many Student Standards provide a framework for inquiry-based learning: Empowered Learner, Digital Citizen, Knowledge Constructor, Innovative Designer, Computational Thinker, Creative Communicator, and Global Collaborator (see Appendix A).

ISTE Standards for Students #1: Empowered Learner
Students leverage technology to take an active role in choosing, achieving, and demonstrating competency in their learning goals, informed by the learning sciences. Students:

   a. Articulate and set personal learning goals, develop strategies leveraging technology to achieve them and reflect on the learning process itself to improve learning outcomes.

   b. Build networks and customize their learning environments in ways that support the learning process.

   c. Use technology to seek feedback that informs and improves their practice and to demonstrate their learning in a variety of ways.

d. Understand the fundamental concepts of technology operations, demonstrate the ability to choose, use and troubleshoot current technologies and are able to transfer their knowledge to explore emerging technologies. (2016)

Empowered learners are decision makers. This shift to a student-centered approach provides students agency in deciding how to attack challenging topics, frame research with their own driving questions, and synthesize new understandings. Do students feel like they have a voice? Students desire to make school relevant and meaningful; they want a place at the decision-making table. Are school decisions based on what's best for the student, or based on what's more convenient for the teacher? Is a culture of student empowerment and openness evident at your school? Take some time to reflect on these questions and bring them to your next faculty meeting.

Culture of Literacy

Creating a culture of inquiry involves immersing students in a print-rich environment to expose them to books for reading pleasure and research. In my school library, we are open flexible hours before and after school, so students can access materials throughout the day. Attractive book displays of informational texts revolve around themes to entice readers to open pages, explore, and learn something new. Probing questions presented alongside interesting exhibits can highlight essential questions of upcoming lessons. Compelling book talks, or ones shared by classmates, are usually enough encouragement for students to read something new. Graphic novels, newspapers, magazines, picture books, and poetry appeal differently to different students. Do your students have access to a wide variety of print materials?

Librarians and classroom teachers can work together to surround students with high-quality publications. Thematic sets can be pulled from the library and brought to the classroom. It is powerful when teachers reference these books during a lesson, and pass them around. Teachers model curiosity when they add their own thoughts to wonder walls (bulletin boards where curious answers are posted) in their classrooms. Challenge your students and visitors to do the same.

District Teacher on Special Assignment (TOSA) and former social studies teacher, Matt Hiefield, had every student in his class create their own digital "curiosity board" using a website called Linoit (linoit.com). Linoit is similar to Padlet (padlet.com); it is like a digital corkboard where you can post images and text and embed videos. If a productive or provocative question came up during a class discussion, Hiefield exclaimed, "Well, that's an interesting question!" and directed his students to add it to their own curiosity boards for later investigation. Occasionally, he had students choose one question to research; they then rearranged their Linoit boards to create mini-digital presentations, with embedded photos or videos alongside content. A gallery walk allowed classmates to view one another's work. What a great way to celebrate curiosity!

Literate environments are not limited to print sources. Engaging digital content, with up-to-date information, is available on many platforms. Starting class with a current-events video from PBS NewsHour Extra, or an engaging article from Newsela, stimulates questions and curiosity. Having students analyze the statistics presented in Gapminder will open up a whole world of questions about population, income, life expectancy, and poverty. Exploring Google Trends will make students wonder about what is happening in the world right this minute. Our students are bombarded with informational facts every day—let's channel that noise into productive curiosity.

Our Task

Innovation cannot thrive if the school culture does not empower students to take risks and allow their questions and curiosity to take center stage. A forward-thinking culture that embodies sharing and openness paves the way for a future in which students' voices are recognized and valued. Our task, as educators, is to surround our children in a print-rich environment while helping them to understand what it means to be a digital citizen of their community. We cannot take this mission lightly. Their future depends on it.

 In the Spotlight

Future Ready Librarian's Framework

The Alliance for Excellent Education (2017) leads the Future Ready Schools (FRS) movement and has a special framework for Future Ready Librarians (FRL) that outlines their role in school transformation (see Figure 1.4). The FRL framework came out of a growing recognition that librarians are "key players" in curating digital resources and empowering students to be creators of knowledge. Librarians are recognized for building instructional partnerships with classroom teachers and designing collaborative spaces.

Mark Ray is the director of innovation and library services for Vancouver Public Schools (VPS). He reports that his district has been focused on "preparing students for both the dynamic now and the evolving next" (2016). He explains the district is exploring the "necessary instructional shifts" toward the Future Ready framework by asking the following questions:

- How can we build both digital citizenship and digital leadership?

CHAPTER 1 | Creating A Schoolwide Culture of Inquiry

- How can we move from consumption to increased creation by students and teachers?
- How can we develop teachers as designers of rich educational experiences for students?
- How can we develop students as owners of their learning?

Ray adds that at VPS, teacher librarians are not merely part of the conversation, "They are involved in the work and leadership as we seek solutions to these and other challenges." If your school district has not taken the Future Ready School pledge, share this information with your district administration: futureready.org.

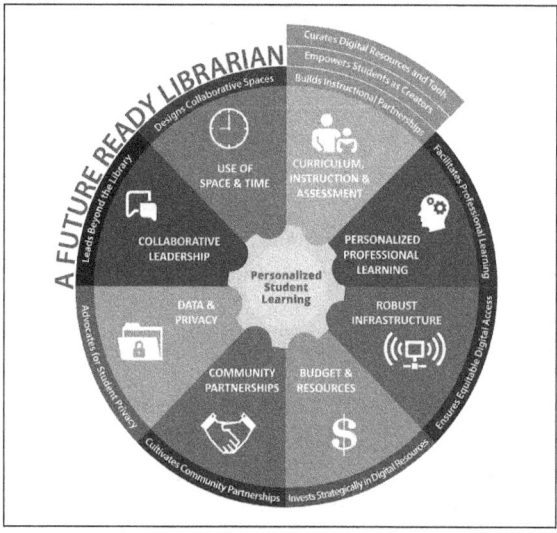

Figure 1.4 Future Ready Librarian's Framework.

20 Inspiring Curiosity

CHAPTER 2

Librarian's Role with Inquiry-Based Learning

Teachers frequently overlook the expertise a librarian can bring to their curriculum. Most often, it's due to time constraints; teachers are busy and don't think to reach out to their librarian for assistance or advice during the preplanning stages. If librarians are informed of the project well in advance, they can create inspirational library displays to pique interest or reserve titles through interlibrary loan. Ultimately, the classroom teacher and librarian are instructional partners who work together to develop assignments that are matched to academic standards.

CHAPTER 2 | Librarian's Role with Inquiry-Based Learning

Developing Collaborative Partnerships

Librarian Rosa Rothenberger and middle-school science teacher Robin Schroeder provide an example of how this type of collaboration can work. They collaborated on a lesson about joints and how they function in the body, specifically helping students identify and describe the purpose of muscles, ligaments, and tendons. Rothenberger, a former science teacher herself, was able to bring knowledge and resources to make the lesson appropriate for a wide range of learners. First, Rothenberger knew her library collection, and shared print and digital resources with the science teacher. When preplanning together, the teachers discussed the process of how students would demonstrate their understanding and the key points of assessment. Rothenberger suggested providing scaffolding to address the needs of all learners, such as a screencast video, a word bank, and diagrams of a chicken wing to assist students during the lab.

During the chicken wing dissection, some students were having difficulty identifying the difference between a ligament and tendon, so they referred to the videos and labeled photos to clear up confusion. Rothenberger encouraged students to take their own photos of the lab and questioned how their observations were informing their understanding. Both teachers guided students, but did not directly instruct them, to make their own conclusions of how a joint works. Because the teachers had worked together in the planning process, they both anticipated when students would struggle with the lab and were able to direct students to print resources and sentence frames to articulate their understanding. The students are the ones who benefit from this type of collaboration. The science teacher is more willing to extend this activity to deepen students' understanding of how the human body works because she knows that she has a collaborator who is willing to help.

Build Relationships

The key to any type of effective collaboration is to focus on relationships. It's very challenging to be involved in inquiry-based lessons if your faculty doesn't trust you. Get to know your faculty on a personal level by showing interest in their lives, asking questions about interests or family, hanging out in the lunch room or at school social events. Especially when you work at a large secondary school, it can take time to build these foundations because teachers are spread across a large building. I make a point to try to eat lunch with the world languages department one week, then with the science teachers the next. These casual conversations are enjoyable, and they send a clear message that you want to know and work with your colleagues—and that is powerful.

Be of Value

Once the personal foundation is built, you can be of value to others. When a new book arrives in the library, send it to a teacher with a note that reads: "This just arrived and I thought it would be perfect for your next unit of study." Or, if your budget allows, purchase some new titles for an upcoming research topic. This demonstrates that you are willing to support the department's inquiry projects. When a new teacher mentions they are struggling with the school's technology programs, offer to stop by and help. This is the perfect time to share the school's databases or the online resources the library has to offer. When you run across a website or a resource that might be valuable to a whole department, send an email with detailed instructions or make a screencast video to teach them the concept. Don't forget to include an offer that you'd be happy to come to their classroom and teach them one-on-one, if that is what they would prefer. Establish yourself as a helpful person.

Show Empathy

Help teachers overcome barriers to inquiry-based learning by being empathetic to their challenges. We all know teachers continue to have demands placed on them year after year. Teachers have new curriculum to learn and learning targets that must be met. Grade-level or subject-level teams may pressure them to keep on track and maintain a curriculum schedule. Acknowledge their challenges of time and pacing, but at the same time, gently remind them that their time and effort focusing on inquiry will pay off with deeper learning for their students. Provide them with articles and research about inquiry-based learning or the importance of preparing students for college-level research. Be an enthusiastic champion of inquiry.

Some teachers might feel unsure about the inquiry process and be uncomfortable assisting students with higher-level research or accessing primary sources. Assure your staff that you will work together and they can learn alongside their students. After presenting a lesson on search strategies, accessing databases, or evaluating sources, I create a short screencast video of the lesson for the teacher to post on a class website or Learning Management System (LMS). Students who were absent can watch the lesson, but it is also helpful for English Language Learners (ELLs) (if you turn on captions) or any student who needs to refer to your instructions throughout the inquiry process. These short video tutorials help teachers improve their research skills, too. (See Chapter 5 for specific tools for making video tutorials.)

Get Involved

I am sure this is a common situation for secondary librarians: A teacher comes to see you at the last minute, asking if students can come to the library to access print and digital resources for a class project that begins tomorrow. Too often, librarians are relegated to only the beginning of an inquiry project by providing sources, or we don't receive the professional courtesy of advance planning. Don't wait—invite yourself to be involved in every aspect of inquiry-based projects—that is what this book is all about!

Suzie Boss, journalist and author of *Bringing Innovation to School: Empowering Students to Thrive in a Changing World* and coauthor of *Reinventing Project-Based Learning: Your Field Guide to Real-World Projects in the Digital Age*, suggests that school librarians should be part of the project-based learning "dream team." Yes, librarians should be involved at the project planning stage, but they can do so much more! Boss lists several ideas in her *Edutopia* article (2013) on being an essential member of the dream team, including:

- Giving feedback during the project planning stage.
- Creating anticipation through book displays or a "curiosity cabinet."
- Guiding research and providing workshops on smarter searching or fair use and copyright.
- Connecting with experts or arrange video conferencing.
- Encouraging teamwork and creativity by reimagining library spaces for teams.
- Displaying "beautiful work" and showcasing student work.

Boss shares,

> I can think of many examples where the project was qualitatively better when the librarian was involved in the planning stage. You are going to get better results by collaborating because one teacher cannot possibly know everything that is out there (2017).

A librarian, for instance, can offer resources that may be unfamiliar to a teacher, such as a graphic novel or video tutorial that matches the curriculum unit. You can offer examples of technology tools that can be used for publishing or encourage the use of primary source materials. Your faculty will be open to new ideas when they know you are on board to help their students be successful with inquiry-based learning. Part of our job is to be cheerleader, and part of our job is to be coach. Understanding that they don't have to jump into large-scale open-inquiry projects from the start might help them get started.

Types of Inquiry

Student autonomy and options to choose their own topics dictate the various levels of inquiry. The most structured type of inquiry, confirmation inquiry, is when the student is provided with the research question and suggested procedures and methods. Structured inquiry differs in that its purpose is to introduce students to conducting investigations or rehearsing a specific inquiry skill. The focus is on the learning process rather than the actual results. During guided inquiry, the question or procedures can still be directed by the teacher, but the students construct explanations and provide evidence to support their conclusions. The final type is open inquiry, where students choose their inquiry questions to conduct their own investigations, curate sources, and design and synthesize their findings to communicate the results (Banchi & Bell, 2008).

In his book, *Dive Into Inquiry* (2016), Canadian English teacher Trev Mackenzie nicely illustrates these levels of inquiry with the metaphor of swimming in a pool. At the beginning of the school year, Mackenzie models inquiry; he has groups conduct research by following similar procedures through a structured program—like everyone synchronized swimming in the shallow end of a pool. This presents opportunities for the librarian to teach specific skills that will be needed later, during independent research. Gradually, control of the learning flips from the teacher to the student until students are "in the deep end of the pool" and free to choose their own topics through open inquiry. Mackenzie cautions teachers from jumping into open inquiry too early because students will not "feel as confident, supported, or empowered through their inquiry journey (p. 27)." Choose the type of inquiry to match the instructional goals of the lesson.

Confirmation Inquiry

Confirmation inquiry is utilized when the goal is to reinforce a previously learned concept. Science teachers often use confirmation inquiry to lead students through an experiment where the students practice a specific scientific skill and the final results are confirmed. Students may need to conduct research to validate the findings of their lab experiment, but often that research is limited or prescribed. Humanities teachers use confirmation inquiry to lead students through a process of examining primary source material and collecting evidence of historical importance.

The school librarian's role during confirmation inquiry may be limited but does not need to be absent. It is best if they are involved in the planning from the beginning because they can make sure the teacher has access to the required text sets, technology software, or data sets. The librarian can provide access to resources or teach skills like data analysis, or copyright and fair use. Though your interaction with students may be limited, everyone benefits when you are involved in the instructional goals. I am always happy to be another set of hands in the classroom and help out when I can. In my school, I am more likely to purchase reference materials for specific lessons if I know they are going to be used by every student in a class.

Structured Inquiry

Structured inquiry revolves around existing curriculum topics that lend themselves to research. Students collect evidence and propose explanations, but the teacher still suggests the essential question and inquiry focus. This type of research is very common in school. The teacher poses a question and provides text sets, and the students read and locate evidence to support their conclusions. Unfortunately, there is very little opportunity for students' curiosity to inform their learning. Librarians and teachers must plan carefully to make sure the provided resources are engaging, informational, at differentiated reading levels, and most importantly, support the goals of the lesson. Providing a graphic organizer for conducting the research is helpful for ELLs or those new to inquiry-based learning. History teacher Alisa Harvey uses the example in Figure 2.1 with her students the first time they begin brainstorming keywords, before they conduct research. Once again, you should be involved in the planning process, especially in locating differentiated material and multimedia options. Librarians can preview Newsela text sets or the Smithsonian's TweenTribune to find engaging articles related to the topic. See Chapter 3 for more resources on current events.

Guided Inquiry

During guided inquiry, the teacher dictates the theme of the research question connected to the essential question of the unit. Students design research plans and procedures to support their curiosity. The inquiry question may be fine-tuned or collaboratively chosen by the class using the Question Formulation Technique (QFT), but usually everyone researches similar topics. (See Chapter 3 for more on QFT.) Since the students have more autonomy during this type of inquiry, librarians work with individual students on evaluating or synthesizing sources. This independence can cause anxiety

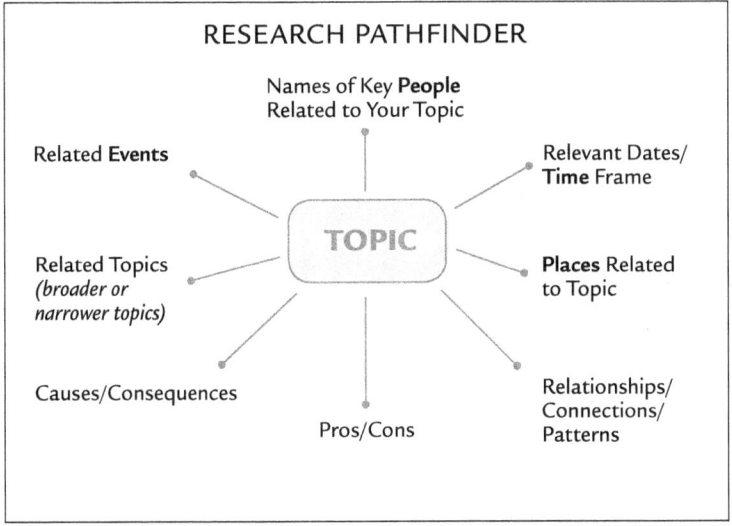

Figure 2.1 Research Pathfinder for History Class.

for some students, particularly if their classmates seem to be finding sources or the student does not have the skill-set to be successful. Librarians can provide personalized learning by offering assistance with many aspects of the research process, such as note-taking, citations, or presentations.

Open Inquiry

Open inquiry is often called free inquiry, passion-based learning, or referenced as "genius hour." It can be the highest level of inquiry because it involves student choice, student-directed involvement, and relevant topics. Note that the subject matter doesn't need to be completely open and some parameters may be helpful for students in selecting their focus. During this type of inquiry, students have the most authentic opportunities to act like scientists, historians, or writers. Students ask questions, design and carry out research, and communicate their results to an authentic audience.

At times, the topic of the inquiry-based lesson will be taken right from curriculum themes. Other times, an experience, current-events topic, novel, or curious question will lead students down the path of exploration. Conceptual questions where students make judgments or speculations based on broader concepts (such as national security, energy, or rituals) are more powerful and complex than specific curriculum events or topics (such as Japanese internment, fuel, or Egyptian pyramids). Researching multiple concepts requires analysis beyond merely reporting basic knowledge and comprehension because these "big ideas" require students to make their own conclusions or synthesize ideas from several disciplines.

The librarian is very involved in all aspects of the research process within open inquiry. Student agency is highly valued. It can be very challenging for the librarian because there are so many unique needs related to time, help, and resources. However, it can also be very rewarding to witness students taking charge of their own learning. To truly impact the student experience, it is imperative that the teacher and librarian are viewed as co-teachers.

Curriculum Planning

In their position statement, *Definition of an Effective School Library Program* (2016), AASL reports that school librarians "serve as an instructional leader, program administrator, teacher, collaborative partner, and information specialist." School librarians and teachers need to collaborate to help students develop information literacy skills and critical-thinking skills to reach their full potential in all curriculum areas.

You might suggest that the classroom teacher plan an instructional unit using the Understanding by Design (UbD) framework, developed by Grant Wiggins and Jay McTighe. Its primary goal is to develop and deepen student understanding: The framework assists educators in applying the process of "backwards design" and focuses the curriculum around essential questions. These "big picture ideas" are used to engage learners and deepen their understanding of important ideas to transfer their learning to new areas (Wiggins, 2011).

I used the UbD lesson template 2.0 (see Figure 2.2) when I collaborated with a history teacher who was struggling to make her lessons more engaging. We really couldn't determine the inquiry activities or experiences until we both clearly understood what would lead to the achievement of the instructional goals. The teacher wanted students to understand the concept of a turning point, and how Enlightenment theories led to new assumptions regarding power, government, and social change. To illustrate the backwards-design plan and thinking, I asked the teacher to consider this prompt:

If the desired end result is for learners to …	Then you need evidence of the learners' ability to …	Then the learning events need to …

The teacher wanted to see evidence that students could locate primary source documents from individuals who lived during the Enlightenment period, then compare and contrast one person's ideas and philosophies with others who were also influential during this time period. Once we both understood what the evidence would look like, I shared an idea I had seen used by another history teacher. That teacher had conducted a European salon-style discussion; each student role-played an individual and spoke in character about their philosophies during a historical salon tea. Students quoted from their person's speeches or documents, and engaged in lively debate with others from the same time period. With the essential plan laid out, both my colleague and I could offer additional suggestions regarding inquiry questions, primary source resources, and follow-up activities.

STAGE 1: DESIRED RESULTS		
ESTABLISHED GOALS	**Transfer**	
	Students will be able to independently use their learning to ...	
	Meaning	
	UNDERSTANDINGS *Students understand that ...*	ESSENTIAL QUESTIONS
	Acquisition	
	Students will know ...	*Students will be skilled at ...*
STAGE 2: EVIDENCE		
Evaluative Criteria	**Assessment Evidence**	
	PERFORMANCE TASK(S):	
	OTHER EVIDENCE:	
STAGE 3: LEARNING PLAN		
Summary of key learning events and instruction:		

Figure 2.2 UbD Lesson Template. Used with permission. Wiggins, G., & McTighe, J. (2005). *Understanding by design* (2nd ed.) Alexandria, VA: ASCD.

Compare the collaboration described above to a scenario when librarians are asked to provide primary source material at the last minute, with no understanding of the teacher's instructional goals. When teachers have a positive collaborative experience, they understand that the time it takes to work together will, in the end, create a rich experience that connects their activities to larger themes, and ultimately improves student learning.

 In the Spotlight

Guided Inquiry Design

Another excellent resource you should share with your faculty is Guided Inquiry Design, a research-based instructional design framework created by Carol C. Kuhlthau, Leslie K. Maniotes, and Ann K. Caspari (2012). Guided Inquiry Design is based on Kuhlthau's model of the information search process, which examined students' "thoughts, feelings, and actions" during the traditional research assignment. Her research demonstrated that a meaningful inquiry question or a thesis statement needs to come toward the middle of the research process rather than at the beginning, which is where traditional research models had it placed (Kuhlthau, 1989). Guided Inquiry Design breaks down the inquiry process and provides inquiry tools that assist students with clarifying their thinking, visualizing ideas, recording their sources, and synthesizing their notes. Librarians can share this framework with secondary teachers. You can examine how inquiry tools (see Chapter 7) are used and view lesson plan templates in *Guided Inquiry Design in Action: High School* (Maniotes et al., 2017). There is also a middle-school version of the book. Librarians are involved in the overall design of the inquiry process but can increase their impact during specific phases (see Figure 2.3).

CHAPTER 2 | Librarian's Role with Inquiry-Based Learning

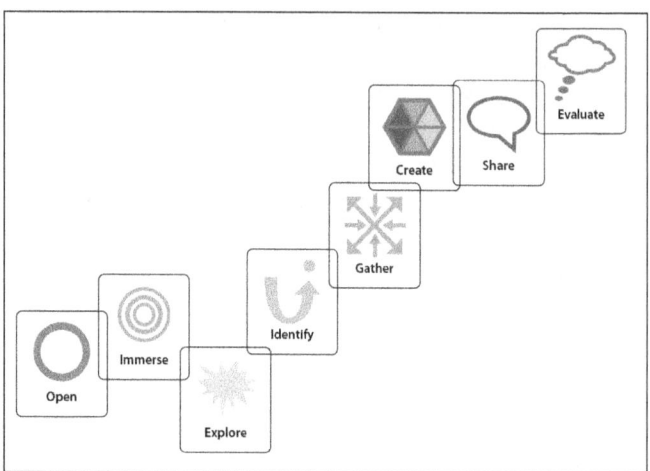

Figure 2.3 Guided Inquiry Design process. Used with permission. Kuhithau, C., Maniotes, L., Caspari, A. (2012). *Guided Inquiry Design: A Framework for Inquiry in Your School.* Santa Barbara, CA: ABC-CLIO.

The idea during the Open phase is to stimulate curiosity and open minds to new thinking and ideas. The opener is designed to spark conversation and focus on a concept or "big idea" to consider a compelling research question. The Immerse phase builds background knowledge and guides students to connect with the content. During the Explore phase, the librarian is very involved as students browse through resources and explore ideas to prepare their inquiry question. Librarians may even provide curated sets of resources, depending on the grade level, to diminish the overwhelming nature of searching far and wide on the internet or library databases. Students often become overwhelmed or uncertain during the Explore phase and are confused how the ideas they have gathered fit together. Educators have reported that it is essential to intentionally design and plan the first three phases of an inquiry to set the students up for success.

The learner pauses to construct a meaningful inquiry question during the Identify phase. They may discuss their ideas with their inquiry circle, or reflect in their journal. During the Gather phase, students may narrow or broaden their focus to curate relevant information from varied sources. Librarians may hold in-depth conferences with students to review their research. Next, students need to interpret and synthesize the information learned and present their findings in the Create phase. The Share phase is the culminating phase of Guided Inquiry Design. Maniotes explains, "Now is the time for students to go back to their initial inquiry question and share what they learned with the community and connect their understanding with the original concept." The final phase, Evaluate, guides students in self-assessment of content learning and process. Notice the "shape" of the Guided Inquiry Design process in Figure 2.3 as it follows the flow of students' emotions and confidence, interest, and learning throughout the inquiry process. Together with the learning team and inquiry tools, students are supported and guided throughout their investigation.

Guided Inquiry Design in Action: High School includes an excellent chapter, written by librarian Heather Hersey, specifically geared toward librarians who want to conduct in-depth conferences. These conferences are used to check in on student research and offer personalized instruction. Many times, there are gaps in their research, or students have quoted material from only one type of source. These conferences can take place anytime throughout the process, but often occur in the Explore or Gather phases (see Figure 2.4). The librarian–student conference focuses on modeling the inquiry stance, teaching of specific research skills, and discussions about feelings and process. Hersey cautions against librarians becoming "source superheroes" during these conferences, but encourages them to provide and model strategies for locating and evaluating meaningful sources. I am guilty of this. In my enthusiasm about the student's research topic, I march them over to the shelves and start handing them books. Instead, I should pause, listen, ask clarifying questions, and try to find out what they have already researched and where they are headed. I need to allow students' questions to dictate what sources they need, and provide them opportunities to refine their search to reveal those sources. Librarians should set clear expectations when scheduling conferences with students. Figure 2.5 is an example of a conference communication plan created by Hersey and her colleagues. Conferencing is an integral aspect of Guided Inquiry Design, and it allows educators to have an impact on student learning.

GUIDED INQUIRY DESIGN FRAMEWORK	
Open	• Invitation to inquiry • Open minds • Stimulate curiosity
Immerse	• Build background knowledge • Connect to content • Discover interesting ideas
Explore	• Explore interesting ideas • Look around • Dip in
Identify	• Identify inquiry question • Pause and ponder • Decide direction
Gather	• Gather useful information • Go broad • Go deep
Create	• Create to communicate • Reflect on learning • Go beyond facts—interpret and extend
Share	• Learn from each other • Share learning • Tell your story
Evaluate	• Evaluate achievement of learning goals • Reflection on content • Reflect on process

Figure 2.4 Guided Inquiry Design Framework. Used with permission. Maniotes, L., Editor (2017). *Guided inquiry design in action: High school.* Santa Barbara, CA: ABC-CLIO.

SETTING CLEAR, EXPLICIT EXPECTATIONS

What you can expect from me:
- An Outlook meeting request for the time that you signed up.
- An email reminder for that meeting.
- I will spend some time researching your topic in advance of our meeting.
- After our conference, I will send you the list of sources that we discussed.

What I expect from you:
(Only spend about fifteen minutes preparing the answers to these questions.)

A **pre-conference email** at least twenty-four hours in advance of our meeting, which will address the following questions:

1. What is your topic or inquiry question?
2. Where are you in your research process?
3. What are gaps in your research?
4. What would you specifically like to focus on during our research conference?

A **post-conference email** within twenty-four hours after our meeting, which outlines the following:

1. Reflect on and explain your key takeaways from the research conference.
2. What do you think will be the most challenging part of this project/process, and how do you plan to tackle it?
3. What are your next steps?

Included in this email are our expectations for rock star researchers:

Rock Star Researchers

Pre-conference Preparation	Student thoughtfully and fully answers each question. Responses show initiative and genuine engagement with topic.
Conference Engagement	Student is actively engaged in learning. Student is curious, asks relevant, thoughtful questions, and takes risks when necessary.
Post-conference Engagement	Student articulates clear takeaways from the conference. Student uses feedback to develop understanding and move his or her research process forward with clear, relevant next steps.

Figure 2.5 Setting Clear, Explicit Expectations. Used with permission. Maniotes, L., Editor (2017). *Guided inquiry design in action: High school.* Santa Barbara, CA: ABC-CLIO.

CHAPTER 3

Inspiring Curiosity

Do teachers at your school discuss ways to cultivate curiosity as an instructional strategy? Ramsey Musallam is a secondary science teacher at Sonoma Academy in Santa Rosa, California, and spends quite a bit of time thinking about his own teaching philosophy. One of the teaching rules Musallam stands by is to unlock and harness the power of student curiosity:

> Rule #1:
> Curiosity comes first. I will try my best to spark authentic student questioning before delivering content.

Curiosity Comes First

Being curious means we are aware there is an "information gap" between what we know and what we don't know. If we have all the knowledge on the topic, we are not as curious as we could be. At the same time, we don't know to be curious if we have no understanding of the topic.

In his book, *Spark Learning: 3 Keys to Embracing the Power of Student Curiosity* (2017), Musallam explains, "Educators need to find that sweet spot where just enough information is removed to pique curiosity and strengthen mental muscle, all while not demotivating students" (p.17) Providing students with some type of artifact, problem, or scenario where information has been strategically removed can spark questioning and promote critical thinking. Ending a video clip just before the conclusion drives students to anticipate the solution themselves. Even providing a scenario where the result is surprising or perplexing can spark curious questioning in search of additional details about the phenomena.

Educators rob students of their natural curiosity when we lecture first and lay out all the necessary knowledge in a specific content area. Musallam suggests that educators prime the brain for meaningful learning—withhold specific information to spark curiosity—then deliver the curriculum material.

Librarian's Role

How can the librarian work with the classroom teacher to cultivate this natural curiosity? As mentioned in the last chapter, it is essential that both educators have a clear understanding about the desired learning outcomes and the evidence that will show that learning has occurred. Effective educators recognize the importance of hooking students at the beginning of a learning experience or inquiry project. The librarian can offer ideas and resources for these opener activities and suggest ways to hold students' interest throughout the unit.

In the UbD curriculum framework (2005), Grant Wiggins and Jay McTighe suggest that careful planning should not only engage learners in the topic but also move students towards "big ideas," essential questions, and performance tasks by design. WHERETO is an acronym that summarizes key elements in a learning plan.

- W **Where** are we going? **Why**? **What** is expected?
- H How will we **hook** and **hold** student interest?
- E How will we **equip** students for expected performances?
- R How will we help students **rethink** and **revise**?
- E How will students self-**evaluate** and reflect on their learning?
- T How will we **tailor** learning to varied needs, interests, and styles?
- O How will we **organize** and sequence the learning?

The UbD framework suggests using the list below to brainstorm possible hooks for your unit design. The next section is a comprehensive listing of powerful openers the librarian can share to inspire curiosity. Allow student choice for:

- Challenge
- Emotional connection
- Experiment—predict outcome
- Humor

- Mystery
- Odd fact, anomaly, counterintuitive example
- Personal experiences
- Problem or issue
- Provocative entry question
- Role play or simulation

Powerful Openers

A powerful opener can set the stage for learning during an inquiry-based lesson, especially when it focuses on a concept or big idea. Openers invite the learner to experience the topic in a new light and set the tone for the whole assignment. An engaging hook helps students connect with the concept and provides background knowledge to encourage discussion. The opener should not just be a "fun activity" but framed around concepts that drive students toward complex abstract ideas that are universal in application, timeless, and grounded in observation (Donham, 2014).

Effective teachers and librarians know the power of a good opener and should spend time discussing and planning how to inspire curiosity and build those connections from the very beginning. Librarians can conduct research to support the learning targets by curating resources such as maps, ebooks, videos, documentaries, and websites to inspire curiosity for the opener. Librarians can also arrange guest speakers or experts, set up simulations in the library, and compile a collection of fiction and nonfiction books to go along with the topic.

The following are examples of how educators have used openers to spark curiosity for inquiry-based lessons.

Video/Film

Language arts teacher Stephanie Lalley uses documentary films from *Independent Lens* to inspire her 11th-grade writing students as an opener for an argumentative essay unit. She shares excerpts from documentary films and encourages students to notice how these films pose a question or concern and then dive deep into the topic. She explains that documentaries are basically "visual essays" in which a director identifies a problem, conducts interviews, and offers commentary or solutions. Lalley has students choose a film where they explore a topic that challenges them to take a position or offer a solution. Documentary films are excellent openers, and they provide an engaging way to gain working knowledge about the topic before beginning research.

Independent Lens (www.pbs.org/independentlens/) is a large showcase of independent documentary films. Students can view a selection of the full-length films online, while other films only provide a preview.

TED Talks (www.ted.com/talks) are inspirational talks on a wide variety of topics. Educators have used TED Talks to inspire, educate, and engage students in deeper thinking.

YouTube and **Vimeo** are video providers where students can find experts in the field, short documentary films, or informational videos. Finding quality videos can be time consuming, but educators can subscribe to educational channels like **Crash Course** (www.youtube.com/user/crashcourse) or Sci Show (www.youtube.com/user/scishow/).

RefSeek (www.refseek.com/directory/educational_videos.html) has a guide to the 25 best online resources for finding free educational videos.

Nonfiction and Literature Novels

At Jesuit High School in Portland, Oregon, librarian Gregory Lum works with English teacher Megan Mathes to use Gene Yang's award-winning graphic novel *American Born Chinese* (2007) as a discussion starter about race and identity. Using a graphic novel allows students to analyze the text and comic design as a way of interpreting the actions of the main character. The comic format provides an interesting forum for addressing a challenging topic. Lum introduces students to the concept of "windows and mirrors" from Rudine Sims Bishop, professor emerita, at Ohio State University. This is the premise that students need to see themselves reflected in diverse literature and films, or use books like windows to look through and see worlds besides their own. Librarians should always be on the lookout for high-quality informational texts and memoirs to be used as hooks for inquiry-based lessons. Illustrated books can help students visualize historical events, understand scientific concepts, or explain cultural differences. Reading a compelling biographical story is not only inspiring, but also educational.

One of the most powerful things a teacher or librarian can do is to cultivate the habit of approaching texts with wonderment and awe. It can be as simple as thinking aloud, "This has got me wondering about …" or "Now I am thinking differently about this character. I used to think … but now I think …" Fiction and nonfiction texts used as openers can invite students to explore important themes or issues that emerge.

> **The Role of Literature in the Inquiry Classroom** (www.alea.edu.au/documents/item/1117) discusses literature as an information source, used to teach questions and stimulate curiosity, and teaching literature with an inquiry stance.
>
> **YALSA Award for Excellence in Nonfiction** (www.ala.org/yalsa/nonfiction) honors the best nonfiction books published for young adults (ages 12–18) every year.

The full List of **Awards given by the American Library Association for Children and Young Adults** (www.ala.org/awardsgrants/awards/browse/bpma/all/cyad?showfilter=no), includes awards such as The Coretta Scott King Books Award, the Pura Belpré Award (Latino), and Outstanding Books for the College Bound and Lifelong Learners.

CommonLit (www.commonlit.org) is a free literacy resource for teachers, grades 5-12.

We Need Diverse Books (weneeddiversebooks.org) is a grassroots organization of children's book lovers that advocates essential changes in the publishing industry to produce and promote literature that reflects and honors the lives of all young people.

Teen Writers

Literacy themes provoke big picture questions about the human existence, explore coming of age issues, or comment on chaos and order. Secondary students may not have the sophistication to recognize and articulate those thoughts on their own. Consider having students read excerpts from published teen writers who explore their own identity and write about their world through first-person essays, spoken word poetry, or editorials. Online magazines that are written by and for teens are great openers.

Rookie Magazine (www.rookiemag.com) is an independently run online magazine and book series. They publish writing, photography, and other forms of artwork by and for teenagers. Contributors and readers are from all over the world.

Germ Magazine (www.germmagazine.com) is an online magazine geared toward girls—high school and beyond. Germ was founded by young adult author, Jennifer Niven, and accepts submissions from readers.

Teen Ink (www.teenink.com) is a national teen magazine, book series, and website devoted entirely to teen writing, art, photos, and forums. Teens can publish their creative work and opinions on issues that affect their lives.

Additional options for teen publishing can be found at www.tellingroom.org/get-published/places-publish.

Social Justice Issues and Service Learning

The National Curriculum Standards for Social Studies includes the "civic ideals and practices" strand as one of its ten themes of social studies, (www.socialstudies.org/standards/strands). This strand includes emphasis on learning how to get involved in influencing public policy. Other strands (culture, time, continuity, and change, people, places, and environment, etc.) are a natural fit in history or social studies classes as openers, but would be powerful in health, science, or leadership classes, too

Secondary school is also a time when students become passionate about social justice issues. Tap into that positive energy and allow students to learn about issues they care about or affect their community. Project-based learning advocate Suzie Boss suggests utilizing topics that give students a chance to solve real problems in their community or champion solutions to a situation that concerns them. Opportunities where students can think critically of how teens can solve problems will empower them to make a difference. Observing the problem first hand, watching a documentary, or reading about a challenge in their community might be enough of a jumping off point to involve students in civic engagement. Social justice issues and current events are natural openers.

Teaching Tolerance (www.tolerance.org) was founded by the Southern Poverty Law Center. It is dedicated to reducing prejudice, improving intergroup relations, and supporting equitable school experiences. Teaching Tolerance provides free educational materials to teachers, as well as free curricular kits. This is a great resource for social justice inquiry projects.

The Global Oneness Project (www.globalonenessproject.org) offers a rich collection of multicultural films, photo essays, and articles that explore cultural, social, and environmental issues accompanied by companion curriculum.

Rethinking Schools (www.rethinkingschools.org) offers publications related to teaching about social issues in a public-school environment. Book subjects range from rethinking multicultural education, the climate crisis, sexism and gender issues, popular culture and media, and more.

Anti-Defamation League Current Events Classroom (www.adl.org/education-and-resources/resources-for-educators-parents-families) has a collection of K–12 curricular, including lesson plans and units that promote critical thinking and assist educators in teaching current-events topics through the lenses of diversity, bias, and social justice. They also have resources for parents, book lists, and educational programs.

DoSomething (www.dosomething.org/us) is an organization whose primary goal is to support the young people who want to make a difference in the world. Students can browse the campaigns or activism projects and get involved in their community.

News Resources

Most teachers develop inquiry topics from curriculum units, but the challenge is to make those topics meaningful and relevant for today's students. A social studies teacher should look for broad, overarching themes to make connections between historical events and today's news. When studying imperialism in a world history class, for example, a teacher may ask, "In what ways do empires gain and use power?" By exploring issues with power in the world today, students can make meaningful connections of how empires rise and fall, and how that may still be happening throughout the world.

Social studies teacher Andrew Brown begins every class with some type of news segment, infographic, or current-event topic. As students watch news clips he asks them, "What additional questions do you have about this topic?" Students have a special journal where they write down at least three questions from what was introduced that day. Then he challenges them to search online and attempt to locate the answers to one of their questions. During this time, students practice and rehearse search and evaluation strategies as they seek their answers. There are many news resources for exploring currents events geared specifically toward students.

> **Newsela** (newsela.com) is a database of current-events articles scaled at five different Lexile reading comprehension levels. Daily articles are grouped by theme (e.g., war and peace, money, kids, science, law, health, arts, sports, opinion). Newsela also offers text sets for science, literature, social studies, and Spanish, as well as a library of factual information with primary source documents.
>
> **The Learning Network** (www.nytimes.com/section/learning) by the *New York Times* offers classroom resources from lesson plans and writing prompts to news quizzes and student contests—all based on the articles, essays, images, videos, and graphics published on NYTimes.com. Features like the Article of the Day, Teenagers in the Times, and STEM articles are great jumping off points for classroom research.
>
> **PBS NewsHour Extra** (www.pbs.org/newshour/extra/) curates news for students and provides teacher resources for the 7-12 grade levels. Articles are organized by themes (arts and culture, economics, ELA, geography, government and civics, math,

media literacy, politics, science, social issues, social studies, technology and world).

CNN10 (www.cnn.com/cnn10) is a daily 10-minute news show from CNN that explains global news to a global audience. The show appears as a daily digital video; it identifies stories of international significance and clearly describes why these stories are making the news, who is affected, and how the event fits into international society.

TweenTribune (www.tweentribune.com) from Smithsonian provides daily AP news articles, Lexile-leveled articles for K–12, self-scoring quizzes, critical thinking questions, Español AP articles, and weekly video and lesson plans.

World-Newspapers (www.world-newspapers.com/index.html) presents links to sources for every country's news. All listed sites are in English and provide free online content.

Science News for Students (www.sciencenewsforstudents.org) offers compelling science articles that are age-appropriate for learners. Each story includes further readings, citations to the original research, power words, and a readability score to ensure the text is accessible to teens.

RadioLab (www.radiolab.org) is a show about curiosity. It is branded as "Where sound illuminates ideas, and the boundaries blur between science, philosophy, and human experience."

Primary Sources

Make learning history come alive by examining primary source documents, videos, and artifacts from a historical era. History teachers have long known the power of using primary source documents to help students examine topics from multiple perspectives and consider their influence on historical issues. Debates and Socratic seminars, in which students must use claims backed by documentary evidence, are valuable activities before diving into research.

> **Library of Congress** (loc.gov/teachers) has put together student discovery ebook sets using historical artifacts and one-of-a-kind documents on topics from history to science to literature. Use the primary source analysis tool when using LOC sources (loc.gov/teachers/usingprimarysources/guides.html).
>
> **DocsTeach** (www.docsteach.org) is the online tool for teaching with documents from the National Archives.
>
> **Digital Public Library of America** (dp.la/primary-source-sets) contains sets designed to help students develop critical thinking skills by exploring topics in history, literature, and culture through primary sources.
>
> **World Digital Library** (www.wdl.org/en) promotes international and intercultural understanding by examining cultural treasures and significant historical documents from all countries and cultures.
>
> The **Reading Like a Historian** (sheg.stanford.edu/rlh) curriculum engages students in historical inquiry. Each lesson revolves around a central historical question and features sets of primary documents designed for groups of students with diverse reading skills and abilities.
>
> **StoryCorps** (storycorps.org) collects stories and interviews from people all over. Primary sources aren't only about historical documents!

Connecting with Experts

Librarian Stony Evans helped connect an eighth-grade science teacher with Joe Serigano, an astronomer and Ph.D. candidate at Johns Hopkins University, through the "Skype a Scientist" program (www.skypeascientist.com). The class composed and sent a list of questions ahead of time, so Serigano could prepare for the Skype session. Students asked questions about Saturn, its moons, his background, and even science fiction movies to see if the ideas presented were possible. After speaking with an expert, students' own questions might drive their inquiry research.

On the **Skype in the Classroom** community page (education.microsoft.com/skype-in-the-classroom/overview), you will find links to Virtual Field Trips, Skype Lessons, Skype Collaborations, Mystery Skype, and Guest Speakers. Skype in the Classroom connects students worldwide in 235 countries and regions and 66 languages. This virtual communication tool offers real-life learning experience while taking students around the world without ever leaving the classroom or library. Combine these activities with Geo Tools (see the "In The Spotlight" section of this chapter) to make powerful connections with geography tools.

Mystery Skype/Hangout is a game invented by teachers and played by two classrooms using virtual communication tools. The aim of the game is to guess the location of the other classroom by asking questions. Students share their culture, and schools form connections while breaking down geographic barriers.

Nepris (www.nepris.com) connects industry professionals with classrooms to bring real-world relevance to what students are learning. Invite subject matter experts to help students understand how curriculum topics are applied in various industries. Presenters can help students with their projects, offer feedback, or just make learning authentic.

Twitter is also a great platform to reach out to experts.

Real-World Science, Math, and Health

Educator Wendy Gorton engaged her students in science and social studies inquiry when she was a teacher-research scientist in the NOAA Teacher at Sea program. Following the learning adventures of teachers is a fabulous opener for science research. Other science teacher education programs include Earthwatch Educator Fellow, PolarHusky Teacher Explorer, National Geographic Challenge Teacher, and NEH Fellow. Engaging science, math, and health openers are valuable and applicable to everyday life.

> **National Institutes of Health** (www.nih.gov/research-training/science-education) provides science education resources for students and teachers.

> Visual data sets or graphs from the **Racial Dot Map** (demographics.virginia.edu/DotMap/index.html), **Gapminder** (www.gapminder.org), **Google Trends** (trends.google.com/trends), or the **Pew Research Center** (www.pewresearch.org) are great jumping-off points for speculation, discussions, and making connections.

> **Real World Math** (www.realworldmath.org) is a collection of free math activities designed for Google Earth. In the virtual world of Google Earth, concepts and challenges can be presented in meaningful ways that portray their usefulness.

> **The Environmental Health Student Portal** (kidsenvirohealth.nlm.nih.gov) explores topics such as water pollution, climate change, air pollution, and chemicals. It is geared toward middle school students and contains links to articles, games, activities, and videos.

Arts and Culture

Amy Burvall and Dan Ryder, authors of *Intention: Critical Creativity in the Classroom* (2017), believe the more students "are invested in their learning and demonstrating their knowledge through creative expression, the more relevant and sticky their newly formed understandings will be" (p. 54). The featured creative experiences for enrichment and exploration found in their book could be powerful openers for inquiry-based learning. From their catalog of critical creativity, **Potent Quotables** asks students to interpret key quotations from notable figures and to demonstrate the depth of their understanding through visual representation for an audience (p. 127). This creative opener will engage students in research, plus it will encourage them to have fun with visual design and photography!

> **Google Arts & Culture** (www.google.com/culturalinstitute) offers diverse art collections from all around the world as well as stories behind historical events. You can also take a tour around historical sites from the ancient and modern world.
>
> **ArtBabble** (www.artbabble.org/educators) provides short video clips showcasing art pieces, techniques, or terminology that can be used to kick off a lesson.
>
> **Wonderopolis** (wonderopolis.org/wonders) poses a curious question every day.

While this list presents many great ideas for opening activities for inquiry, educators should constantly be on the lookout for engaging stories to inspire curiosity. Whenever you come across an interesting phenomenon, a clip from a movie, or read about a crisis in your community, bring it to your students and ask, "What do you think of this? Why should we care?" If students feel that you value their opinions, they will work hard to show you what they know. Sometimes the inquiry-based lesson is spontaneous and organic, other times the teacher and librarian can craft experiences that present opportunities for students to think critically and solve problems.

Problem-Based Learning

Tap the collective knowledge of the group when posing a problem that requires teamwork and research. Problem-based learning is different than other openers because, when the teacher provides the problem, each group may proceed through the inquiry lesson using different approaches. Math teacher Dan Meyer's *Three-Act Math* (2011) visually poses a story or problem using a video or visual prompt. Students then determine what information is needed to solve the problem. Finally, the problem is solved but sets up a sequel or extension. In problem-based learning, simulations or realistic scenarios are also used to immerse students in real-world problems, with students taking on active roles as engineers, economists, stockbrokers, or researchers. Scientific or math problems mimic the work of professionals and engage students in work that matters.

Dr. Paul Hampton teaches ninth-grade physics at Sunset High School and usually begins with a curious phenomenon. Hampton explains that our brains are wired to anticipate an outcome, and when an experiment turns out differently than we expected, it catches our attention and provokes questions. During one lesson on kinetic energy, Hampton asked a student to stand on a desk and drop a piece of paper to the ground. It fluttered to the floor, which was expected. Hampton wanted students to truly understand the concept of kinetic energy and form their own conclusions rather than learning and memorizing a formula. Traditionally, science students would read about different forms of energy in a textbook, listen to a lecture, or memorize the equation for kinetic energy. You remember it, right? Kinetic energy is directly proportional to the mass of the object and to the square of its velocity ($K.E. = 1/2\, m\, v^2$). After several paper drop attempts, Hampton asked students to work with a lab group to maximize the kinetic energy of the piece of paper, but they could not change the mass. This scenario led groups to all kinds of discussion about changing the variables and building prototypes, and new questions developed as they defined the boundaries of the problem.

Students were encouraged to go online and watch videos or research concepts of aerodynamics. Dr. Hampton believes in the power of curiosity and models the spirit of science inquiry in his classroom. You will rarely find him lecturing for long periods of time or see his students filling out worksheets. Instead, he asks his students to be curious observers and thinkers. Later in the period he poses the question, "How do you know you increased the kinetic energy?" This leads to additional data collection as students record observations on iPads, using an app called Seesaw, and submit drawings, videos, and observations to Hampton for review. During a debriefing conversation, student comments and questions about the effect of changing the variables clearly demonstrate their understanding. Educators should take time to observe a science lesson and consider how a curious phenomenon could be used to inspire curiosity in their particular subject area.

Design Thinking

Design thinking is a mindset and approach to learning, collaboration, and problem solving. The Teaching and Learning Lab from Harvard Graduate School of Education defines the design process as "revolving around a structured framework for identifying challenges, gathering information, generating potential solutions, refining ideas, and testing solutions." Stanford's d.school places "empathy" at the beginning of its design process (see Figure 3.1). They stress the importance for design thinkers to empathize with the people they're designing for to understand their needs, thoughts, emotions, and challenges. Only then can potential solutions be researched, suggests the K–12 Lab Network at Stanford University. The K–12 Lab Network offers design challenges and lessons that could be used as inquiry openers. Review the books in Appendix B for design challenges that could be utilized as powerful openers.

A combination of design thinking and a library makerspace provides students with materials they can use to test, refine, and design a prototype that solves a problem. This new type of invention literacy is clearly spelled out in the ISTE Standards for Students:

> Students develop and employ strategies for understanding and solving problems in ways that leverage the power of technological methods to develop and test solutions. (2016)

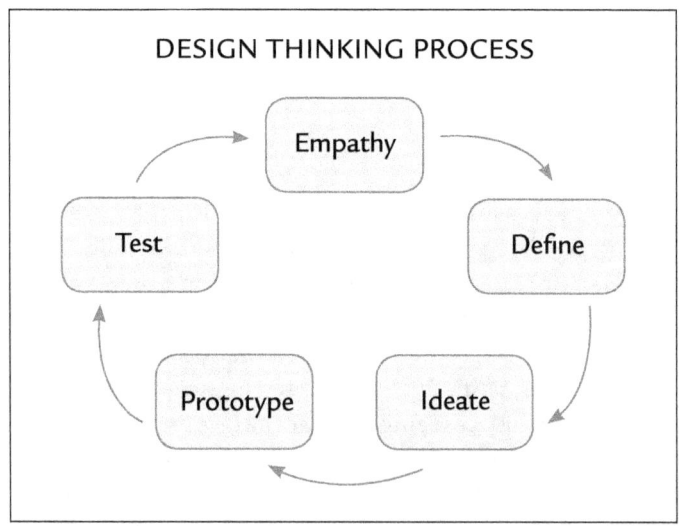

Figure 3.1 Design Thinking Process.

Library makerspaces provide equitable access for all students to be inventive and employ design thinking processes as they build and create. Librarian Colleen Graves states,

> Another reason I love the invention literacy movement is that it directly relates to making our kids active producers of our world and not passive consumers. ... I want to see kids that are curious and want to know how stuff works because they want to make the world a better place. It's one of my main goals in my library makerspace, and I love to see these ideas take hold of my students and see the change it enacts upon them! (2016)

Every Monday during lunch, my high-school library hosts #MakerMonday. This is an exploratory invitation for students to visit the Apollo Press Student Publishing Center and "play" with our creative design tools or try out a design-thinking challenge. It is fun and completely optional. Students design and create objects to be printed on the 3D printer or use the 3D doodling pen to build sculptures. Students race Spheros or program them to complete a miniminigolf course. Some enjoy creative crafts and bookbinding, while other students experiment with TouchCast Studio and our green screen. My goal in having this creative space is for teens to meet other teens who like to "make things," but also to inspire them to use these tools for future academic projects. It seems to be working because now teachers bring students to tour the Publishing Center, and I have a chance to pitch stop-motion videos, handmade journals, paper circuits, and a host of creative ideas for school inquiry projects.

John Larmer, editor in chief of the Buck Institute of Education (BIE), refers to problem-based, challenged-based, designed-based, place-based, and passion-based learning as "modern versions of the same concept" but each has its own "distinct flavor" (2015). Each have aspects of inquiry-based learning and, while several may have similar features, their distinctions generally fit within certain disciplines or outcomes. Inquiry-based learning focuses on the driving question and the reflection of the learning process, while problem-based learning focuses more on sharing information to an authentic audience. Problem-based learning often uses cases studies of scenarios to spark creative problem solving. Engaging students and impacting student learning—no matter what you call it—is the ultimate goal.

Project-Based Learning

People Leading Across City Environments (PLACE) is an initiative of the Catlin Gabel School in Portland, Oregon. Wanting to tackle real-world problems, students from Catlin Gabel met with city officials to learn about issues in their community and offer solutions from a teen perspective. Students researched and produced high-quality reports incorporating data they gathered and analyzed from conducting community research. PLACE now offers a resource guide *Make your PLACE: A Guide to Facilitating Youth Civic Leadership* (2017) to reach schools across the United States. Ideas focus on everything from school-based bike share programs, youth involvement in teen-friendly places, food insecurity, to neighborhood walkability. Interest is growing in having secondary students use service learning, and the community as context, for more authentic inquiry experiences.

Suzie Boss shares the story of PLACE as an example of "gold standard" project-based learning. According to BIE, gold standard project-based learning has three parts. A key aspect is to focus on student learning goals. Key knowledge, understandings, and success skills are at the center of effective projects. Just as in the PLACE example, students investigate real-world issues and work together to gather information, to solve a problem, and make a difference.

Essential project design elements outline what is necessary for a successful gold standard project. Start with a challenging problem or question, and involve sustained inquiry using traditional research methods as well as field-based interviews with experts. Problems need to be big enough to matter, but actionable enough that students feel they can make a difference. Projects can have an authentic context, involve real-world processes or tasks, lead to a real impact, or have personal authenticity. When students have some input and control over a public product, they feel a sense of ownership. Finally, critique and reflection on both the content knowledge and skill development helps students solidify what they have learned and experienced. Boss suggests that educators should look at their curricular map and find units where students can go deeper and become active researchers.

Finally, gold standard projects use project-based teaching practices. Teachers are a "guide on the side" but continue to design and plan the project-based learning context. Projects are carefully aligned to standards as teachers and librarians focus on building the culture to promote independence and growth. They employ a variety of strategies by scaffolding student learning and use formative and summative assessments. The project-based learning teacher is engaged alongside their students and coaching them when necessary (Larmer, Mergendoller & Boss, 2015).

Boss is often asked how teachers can find authentic projects. She suggests thinking about the discipline you are teaching and asking how professionals in that field share their ideas with the world. If you teach history, for example, consider what do historians do? Historians create museum exhibits, they write books, they publish journal articles, they produce documentaries, they testify in public about events, they render opinions, and so on. Together with a real purpose, any one of these ideas could point

CHAPTER 3 | Inspiring Curiosity

the direction of a project, and it will feel authentic for that discipline. Librarians can play an important role in project-based learning, especially if they are involved in the planning from the beginning. They can offer resources the classroom teacher may not have considered, and they can help arrange speakers or people to interview. Boss also suggests inviting interested community members—especially anyone who was interviewed—to view the final exhibits or presentations. Students will want the information to be accurate if the audience is knowledgeable and authentic.

Northwest ecology teacher Lindsey Mockel from Sunset High School knows that having her students do the "real work of scientists" is important in making learning approachable and relevant. Mockel partners with Clean Water Services and Dr. Patrick Edwards, along with graduate and undergraduate students from Portland State University, to collect data about water quality and microscopic organisms in the Tualatin River watershed. Mockel's classes visit Gale's Creek several times in the fall semester to collect data. Students are challenged to set up an experiment where they determine if the stream flow affects algae growth on rocks in the stream and count the presence of scraper bugs. Debris in the stream is conducive to microscopic habitat and a healthy food chain. In the spring, students have a chance to run an experiment of their choosing focusing on the underlying ecological relationship. Science teachers, for years, have utilized inquiry-based lessons with students to examine the data and make conclusions based on the evidence. Dr. Edwards is using the data collected by the students to do a longitudinal study of Gales Creek. The fact that the students add their data with the Tualatin Creek watershed researchers requires students to be scientists and make sure their conclusions are solid. Deep learning occurs when students have opportunities to be scientists and research why the evidence supports, or does not support, the conclusion based on scientific data.

Geography Tools

Students can use the web-based Google Earth (earth.google.com/web) to travel the world and explore new places. Using Google Streetview, they can see in 3D places such as exotic cities, famous landmarks, and historic buildings. Photospheres are 360-degree photos that provide real views of our world—even the International Space Station! A great way to pique students' interest in exotic places is by using a feature called Voyager. Voyager is a collection of map-based tours written by Google Earth partners that provide guided stories on topics such as travel, culture, nature, and history.

There is power in students creating their own maps to help them visualize information or tell a story. Students can use Google Tour Builder (tourbuilder.withgoogle.com) to write place-based stories that follow a journey on a map. The addition of multiple images and videos can make the journey come to life. Google My Maps (www.google.com/maps/d/u/0) allows multiple students to collaborate on an interactive map together.

How about taking students on virtual field trips to engage their curiosity? Google Expeditions allows students to swim with the sharks, visit outer space, or walk through a museum without leaving the classroom. Each participant will need a mobile device that fits into a VR viewer. Teachers then can choose from over 500 Google Expeditions (mrcaffrey.com/google-expeditions-world-map) to share with their students. Get some lesson ideas at www.tes.com/teaching-resources/google.

Here are some additional geography resources to explore:

National Geographic Society Google Earth (www.nationalgeographic.org/education/google-earth)

Google Earth Education (www.google.com/earth/education)

> Google Cultural Institute (virtual tours in museums) (www.google.com/culturalinstitute/beta)
>
> Smarty Pins (trivia) (smartypins.withgoogle.com)
>
> GeoGuessr (geoguessr.com)
>
> Google Lit Trips (www.googlelittrips.org)
>
> Real World Math (www.realworldmath.org)

AR apps (show a view of the real world in front of you, then put a layer of information, including text and/or images, on top of that view):

> Quiver (3D coloring) (www.quivervision.com)
>
> Anatomy 4D (anatomy4d.daqri.com)
>
> Elements 4D (chemistry) (elements4d.daqri.com)
>
> Aurasma (AR creation tool) (www.aurasma.com)

VR apps (show a completely different reality than the one in front of you; may be artificial, such as an animated scene or an actual place that has been photographed):

> VR Lessons by ThingLink (demo.thinglink.com/vr-edu)
>
> Google Streetview (www.google.com/streetview)
>
> View Master (www.view-master.com)
>
> Tilt Brush (www.tiltbrush.com)

 In the Spotlight

Geo Tools for Inspiring Inquiry
Seventh-grade social studies teacher Micah Shippee worked with over 100 students at Liverpool Middle School on the Liverpool Cemetery Mapping project (2015). Students

researched, photographed, and digitally labeled gravestones in the Liverpool Cemetery and then completed a custom Google Map, complete with historical profiles for over thirty gravesites (goo.gl/8jXW1F). The project was then converted with Wikitude (www.wikitude.com), an AR program that used the student-created Google Map content. Through the use of the free Wikitude app installed on a device, visitors to the cemetery can determine the location of each gravesite, how far they have to walk to see them, and the historical profiles for each site. You can be assured those middle-school students took their families to see the virtual walking tour they created.

The advancement of geo technology tools makes place-based learning more of a possibility than ever before. Students can virtually visit locations and view the landscape, culture, and environment of areas they are studying. Immersive technology tools provide interactive experiences where students can use AR or VR software to "place" themselves into simulations or walkthroughs. Mapping software, like GE Teach (www.geteach.com), developed by high-school geography teacher Josh Williams, allows students to compare two maps side-by-side as a way compare data sets from physical geography (physical features, land temperature, precipitable water, carbon dioxide, and so on) and human geography (population density, economy, human development, etc.). Geo tools are powerful openers because they invite students to view the world in a new dimension, and they stimulate curiosity and questions. These resources are wonderful for social studies teachers, but they are applicable in many subject areas, such as world languages, health, and science.

CHAPTER 3 | Inspiring Curiosity

CHAPTER 4

Developing Effective Questions

Student-generated questions are at the heart of inquiry learning. Not only do they drive the inquiry process, but they also provide evidence of students' understanding. Questions that are open, provocative, arguable, reflective in nature, and have no simple, singular answer will ultimately result in the creation of additional questions that will sustain inquiry. Educators can help students understand that their curiosity is an essential ingredient in fine-tuning their question.

CHAPTER 4 | Developing Effective Questions

Question Formulation Technique

The Question Formulation Technique (QFT) was developed by Dan Rothstein and Luz Santana, coauthors of *Make Just One Change: Teach Students to Ask Their Own Questions* (2011). The QFT assists students in learning how to develop and refine their own questions and create research or discussion strategies. Librarians and teachers can use this technique to engage students in a new unit, assess students' knowledge of topics discovered in class, or check for understanding. Teachers have used this technique at the end of a comprehensive unit to propel students into a new inquiry by asking, "What's next?"

Here are the basic steps of the QFT:

1. Teachers design a question focus.
2. Students use a protocol to produce questions without the teacher.
3. Students improve their questions (work with closed-ended and open-ended questions).
4. Students prioritize their questions.
5. Students and teachers decide on next steps to guide discussion.
6. Students reflect on what they have learned.

I watched a video of the QFT and was inspired to try it with my students. At the time, I was teaching a multimedia/web design course and used the technique to engage students in the impact of digital manipulation in today's society. I showed students a series of images and asked them to vote whether they believed the images had been digitally altered. Students were able to correctly identify several of the fabricated images but were surprised by some—specifically, a photo of students cheering at a university football game. The photo had been digitally altered to include a black student so the crowd appeared more diverse. While discussing this controversy, students raised additional concerns about the ethics of digital manipulation.

I decided to use the QFT and have students work in small groups to brainstorm questions about digital manipulation and its use today. We used the four rules for producing questions: (1) Ask as many questions as you can; (2) Do not stop to judge, discuss, edit, or answer any question; (3) Write down every question exactly as it was asked; and (4) Change any statements into questions. After brainstorming, we reviewed whether their questions were closed or open-ended and discussed the advantages and disadvantages of both. Groups then edited their questions to be open-ended and considered if they should be reworked. Students then worked together to prioritize which questions they wanted to investigate.

The discussion and debate among students at this time was eye-opening, and most of the groups decided on different issues as their top priority. Groups shared their top questions with the whole class then once again evaluated their list to see if any of their opinions changed. Finally, each group settled on a specific question to drive their research. By the time the students had completed the QTF, previous background knowledge about the topic was revealed, but more importantly, students were eager to discover real answers to their questions. They were primed to begin research.

For an exit ticket activity, I asked students to think about the entire exercise and tell me what they learned by producing, improving, and prioritizing their questions. One student initially thought she understood why people digitally altered their photos, but after the brainstorming exercise, she realized she hadn't considered certain situations. This student was open to new information as she began her research because the QFT exercise challenged her initial assumptions about a topic.

Students Ask the Questions

Students are in charge when they use the QFT. They ask the questions, they improve those questions through discussion and editing, prioritize the results, and make all the decisions. The teacher facilitates the process and does not drive it forward with her own predetermined set of questions. This can be challenging for teachers who are used to guiding class discussions or directing the path of research. The process can also be difficult for students at first, but the processing time will shorten as students become more comfortable with the procedures. We want students to ask questions to which they don't know the answers or that cannot be Googled. The time it takes to develop purposeful and authentic questions will pay off as they begin research.

Students will become more engaged in the inquiry process when they learn how to ask powerful questions, and the whole experience becomes transformational. Rothstein and Santana state, "When students know how to ask their own questions, they take greater ownership of their learning, deepen comprehension, and make new connections and discoveries on their own" (2011). Those new connections are the transfer of learning that is the basis of authentic, deep knowledge.

When discussing how their Writing 121 students chose their topics for a nine-week research essay, English teachers Rebecca Larson and Tara Slaughter highlighted the need to create time and space for interesting topics and questions to be fully realized. Using techniques found in *The Curious Researcher: A Guide to Writing Research Papers* (Ballinger, 2012), the teachers pushed student curiosity and questioning with brainstorming activities. Students described found objects using a technique called "The Myth of the Boring Topic," and they collaborated on extensive interest surveys. The students laughed, debated topics, and tested the teachers to see if *any* topic was open for discussion. Slaughter reported that some students were nervous about choosing the right topic. She reassured her students that it was more about asking the right questions about a topic—and then to *keep* asking questions until they hit upon one that appealed to them. Larson and Slaughter had students look at their initial research questions through different lenses. For example, the inquiry question might focus on an explanation (sense-making questions), testing assumptions (hypothesis testing), or whether there is a cause and effect (relationship/analyzing focus) for a topic. Once the students focused their research, the teachers reassured them that research questions shift and change as new evidence and ideas lead them down different paths of inquiry.

Develop a Culture of Thinking Using Visible Thinking

It can be challenging for students to process all of their thoughts, ideas and emotions throughout the inquiry process. They may have developed better questions, but how do they now internalize what they are reading and discussing? The central idea of Visible Thinking from Harvard's Project Zero (2017) is very simple: making thinking visible. The goals are to develop students' thinking skills and to deepen subject-area content learning through documentation. Thinking dispositions refers to "being curious, having concern for truth and understanding, and having a creative mindset." Librarians and teachers should consider using Visible Thinking routines for connecting prior knowledge or organizing ideas through concept mapping. These protocols help students develop patterns of thinking. Here are a few core thinking routines (available at goo.gl/cu4Wrl):

- *What Makes You Say That?* Interpretation with justification routine.
- *Think Puzzle Explore.* A routine that sets the stage for deeper inquiry.
- *Think Pair Share.* A routine for active reasoning and explanation.
- *Circle of Viewpoints.* A routine for exploring diverse perspectives.
- *I used to Think ... Now I think ...* A routine for reflecting on how and why our thinking has changed.
- *See Think Wonder.* A routine for exploring works of art and other interesting things.
- *Compass Points.* A routine for examining propositions.

Other thinking routines from Visible Thinking focus on understanding, fairness, truth, and creativity. As a librarian, I especially like the routine "I used to think ... but now, I think ..." because it explores how or why a student's idea has changed over time. This routine could be used as students reflect on how their own learning changed after conducting research.

The creative routine called "Step Inside: Perceive, Know, Care About" helps students explore different perspectives and viewpoints as they imagine things, events, problems, or issues differently. This routine is useful to engage students' creative thinking as they immerse themselves in characters and look at a situation from different points of view.

When students develop their own research questions and document their thinking in a creative manner, they take agency of their own learning. Inquiry learning that incorporates student choice provides pathways for students to genuinely invest themselves in quality work that matters. Choice assists students in finding their own passion, developing an authentic voice, and refining their personal learning style.

Genius Hour

Genius Hour is an inquiry-driven, passion-based strategy designed to engage and empower students. Dedicated time is scheduled weekly, and students are able to learn about and create whatever they want. Genius Hour, often used in middle schools, allows students to develop their own inquiry stance based on their interests, passions, or even things that they are just wondering about. Personalized learning and personal choice is at its central core.

Two librarians from two different states organized GeniusCon, a virtual conference inspired by Genius Hour (Michaelson, 2014). They wanted to celebrate solutions kids find to the problems faced in today's schools. Librarians Sherry Gick and Matthew Winner presented their students with the following prompt: "If you could change one thing about your school, what would you do?" This project attracted first graders through college students from across the nation; they suggested ways to end bullying, improvements to dress code and cell phone policies, changes to lunch menus, plans for after-school clubs, proposals for school-based gardens, and extensions of library book checkout times. Gick and Winner coordinated Google Hangouts for the GeniusCon as a way to connect classrooms and hear kids of all ages using their "genius" to make the world a better place.

CHAPTER 4 | Developing Effective Questions

In his blog post, "The Research Behind Genius Hour and Choice in the Classroom," A. J. Juliani offers a fantastic list of research supporting the benefits of Genius Hour. His post also includes books to read, links to other teachers' Genius Hour work, and connections to Common Core State Standards (2017b). Thousands of librarians and teachers around the world are conducting Genius Hour successfully; find examples by searching #GeniusHour on Twitter and by checking out The Global Genius Hour Project wiki (theglobalgeniushourproject.wikispaces.com) and the Genius Hour LiveBinder (www.livebinders.com/play/play/829279).

Librarian's Role

Instructional strategies like the QFT, Visible Thinking, or Genius Hour provide librarians with tools and resources to offer when collaborating with classroom teachers. Librarians should ask ourselves, "How can I be more involved in helping my students develop solid questions for inquiry and research?" School librarians can offer personalized learning for individual students who are struggling with their inquiry questions, or we can be a sounding board to help students broaden or narrow their ideas. Librarians can assist with identifying researchable topics for students. Not only do we know our own print collection in the library, we can also direct students to appropriate digital resources to spark topic ideas. I often encourage students to browse lists of controversial topics in the Gale Cengage database, Opposing Viewpoints in Context. Students can view a list of topics on various social issues, from capital punishment to immigration to marijuana. One advantage of doing this, I share with students, is that you know you have a starting place to begin your research.

Librarians can pull together a cart of books for students to browse when they are still in the exploratory stages. Librarians can give book talks and read segments to inspire curiosity. Consider creating displays in the library that spur students' questions about subjects they may have never previously considered. Too often, students know how to be recipients of learning, but they don't know how to contribute and be active learners. You can be another adult in a student's life who challenges them to think for themselves and examine topics that interest them. Librarians can encourage students to branch out and conduct interviews or visit museums to further research. I like to challenge my students by saying, "Don't think like a historian; be a historian!"

A student-centered school library helps students engage in inquiry-based learning by being an inclusive, community space that enables a variety of learning and equitable access to all kinds of resources. An effective library is continuously assessed and evaluated to make sure it meets the needs of the school community and has the resources and personnel to support inquiry-based learning. Here are some aspects you should consider and evaluate for your own library:

Physical resources. Evaluate the depth in your collection of printed materials and objects.

Digital resources. Promote and evaluate resources available through the library's online presence.

Local resources. Connect with references to sites, places, or events that can support inquiry.

People. Identify access to experts whose knowledge and insights can inspire or inform inquiry.

CHAPTER 4 | Developing Effective Questions

Mentor Groups

Inquiry circles are another effective instructional strategy where librarians can be involved in the inquiry process. Writing teachers Rebecca Larson and Tara Slaughter used "mentor groups" when their senior Writing 121 students were conducting a nine-week research investigation for a dual-credit writing course. Mentor groups are similar to inquiry circles, but they also include an outside adult who is interested in their topic. Students from different course sections were placed in mentor groups, based on common themes. As the school librarian, I was a mentor for a group of students whose topics had a historical connection. Other mentors from our school included interested teachers, administrators, parents, and district educators. The mentor groups met several times throughout the inquiry process.

Initially, I met with my mentor group to hear about their inquiry topic, why they chose it, and the direction of their research. I went with classes on a field trip to visit the local university library. While there, I directed group members to discuss their topic with the academic librarian, request interlibrary loans, or access the university databases. Later, our group met, and the students discussed challenges and successes with the research process. Students were preparing to create displays about their topics, and this gave me an opportunity to talk about their conclusions and review their two-minute speeches. After the presentations, the students were ready to synthesize their notes from sources and write the research essay. The mentor groups became a forum for sharing ideas, a sounding board for asking clarifying questions, and an avenue for sustaining motivation and excitement during the process. Not all mentor groups were as effective as ours, but conversations between interested adults and students can be a valuable experience.

In the Spotlight

In the Spotlight: Technology Tools for Inquiry

Give students ample time and space for unusual ideas to surface while they use brainstorming or organizing tools during the inquiry process. The goal when using technology is to stimulate creative thinking, provide access for collaboration, and make editing and revising easy.

Writing tools allow students to combine text and/or images, record thoughts, or organize information:

    Google Keep (www.google.com/keep)

    Microsoft OneNote (www.onenote.com)

    Seesaw (web.seesaw.me)

Brainstorming tools capture ideas and thinking and provide space for collaboration:

    Padlet (padlet.com)

    Linoit (en.linoit.com)

    Mindmeister (www.mindmeister.com/education-software)

Drawing apps work well for sketch noting, as interactive whiteboards, or for diagraming ideas:

    Paper by 53 (www.fiftythree.com)

    Explain Everything (explaineverything.com)

    Notability (gingerlabs.com)

Notes and mind-mapping tools document creative thinking and decision making:

    Popplet (popplet.com)

CHAPTER 4 | Developing Effective Questions

Post-it (www.post-it.com/3M/en_US/post-it/ideas/plus-app)

Lucid Chart (www.lucidchart.com)

CHAPTER 5

Diving Into The Research Process

Tasha Bergson-Michelson, instructional and programming librarian at Castilleja School, observes that educators often say secondary students either have a natural ability to search—or not. Yes, our secondary students rely on Wikipedia too much, and they complain they can't find anything when, in reality, they only looked at the first few Google results. Understanding how to design an effective search strategy is challenging to teach because the practice and rehearsal of those strategies take time to perfect. Bergson-Michelson, also a former Google Search Educator, uses a creative way to engage students in problem solving by having her students "imagine the perfect source." She encourages students to "pull a picture of a source into their mind and

Inspiring Curiosity 77

try to imagine what that perfect source would look like"—then sketch it (Bergson-Michelson, 2017). Using only their imagination, students predict the page title, the possible URL, and sketch how the site is organized with potential headings and subheadings. She then asks students to predict what content will be on the page and what type of keywords they will see. Students write captions for one of the images and include names, descriptions, or dates.

Imagine the Perfect Source

Bergson-Michelson reports the benefit of this exercise is that it engages students in creative thinking, emphasizes what they already know about the topic, and is something that everyone can accomplish. The activity shows students have prior knowledge within themselves that they can draw on to imagine sources and begin their initial search. This activity would be beneficial for students needing exposure to new terminology and creative thinking, and it could be extended by sharing sketches with small groups. Once students begin locating information during their background knowledge searches (also known as "stepping stone searches"), students can add additional terms, names, places, and terminology to their sketches to use during keyword searches. Bergson-Michelson notes that imagining a perfect source engages prior knowledge so students can be effective users of "predictive search." She teaches students to ask themselves the following three questions even before they begin a search with a search engine or database.

When I run the search, what do I expect to appear? Too often search terms have multiple meanings and students become confused when unrelated sources appear in the search results or the listing is too vague. There is a huge difference between searching for a term and being confused about the search results—and really imagining, "What did I anticipate?" Students enter a metacognitive mindset and can evaluate the results by asking themselves, "What happened, and what should I do next?" This is a more active method of doing research. It builds curiosity for students to see if they were right and also empowers them as researchers to think critically about their topic.

When I click on this link, what do I expect to see? Too often students start clicking on the links in the search results and become frustrated when there are too many results or the results seem unrelated. They give up. Students who skim easily have an easier time anticipating what the search results might be. Students with lower reading skills or ELLs need more practice in predicting what the result might be *before* selecting the link. Used as a group activity, students review and evaluate one search result. Students vote (before selecting the link) whether they think the link will be helpful or valid based on the information provided. This activity helps students predict and evaluate the search results versus looking through every single link.

When I find this answer, what do I expect it to look like? Encourage students to evaluate the terms they are using in their search. Is the term they are using a common one, such as *drones* versus a term specific to that discipline, such as *unmanned aerial vehicles*? A stepping-stone resource can provide synonyms or discipline-based terminology that will be described in academic terms. Different tones or registers of the same term can also lead to varied results. For example, *Popo* is a slang term for police and the results for that search will have a different slant or bias than searching *police officer*. Students also search on a term they use, such as *undocumented worker*, and will miss different points of view because they are not aware of the political nature of some terminology. Sharing search terms with inquiry circles can help students receive feedback to see if they are on track.

Librarians looking for help in teaching about search should listen to the archive of Bergson-Michelson's webinar "'Imagine Your Perfect Source': Strategies for Cultivating Expert Researchers" from EdWeb (2017). In addition, Joyce Valenza, assistant professor of teaching at Rutgers University School of Information and Communication and blogger for School Library Journal, authored a blog post where she shares 11 secret strategies for serious searchers (2017). One example, citation chaining, is the process of mining the list of references on one source to look for additional useful resources. Valenza's strategies and other search lessons need to be intentionally taught and practiced by secondary students to prepare them for academic research.

Teaching Search

Google has a search education site (www.google.com/intl/en-us/insidesearch/searcheducation) that provides a wide variety of lessons such as using the advanced search tool, site searching, and unique search parameters such as a wildcard or Boolean operators. Helpful techniques such as reverse image search, advanced image filters, or search by file type are unknown to many students. Our students need to learn the difference among standard search results, sponsored content, and related searches. Too often we assume our secondary students are proficient in search because they use electronic devices all the time—academic search is something else. Librarians may want to choose lessons (categorized by level of expertise: beginner, intermediate, or advanced) and incorporate them throughout the inquiry process.

Another resource by Google Search Education is a set of challenges called "A Google a Day." These activities can be used to help students practice their search skills surrounding questions about culture, geography, history, and science. For example, one challenge asks, "Every national flag in the world shares a common geometric characteristic, except for one country. Which country is it?" Hints are given to help students get started and search strategies are shared alongside the answer. My students have found them to be fun and love to race to find the answers first. Teachers and librarians will find these challenges helpful when teaching and modeling specific search strategies, or using them as class openers.

As librarians, we are tasked with providing instruction with databases versus using the open web. We set up a false pretense if we claim that database articles are more "reliable" simply because they have been previously published. Bergson-Michelson explains student researchers need to focus on "what variety of *evidence* do they need—found through what *variety* of sources (2017)" versus just the number of required sources. The emphasis is to think critically about *what type of source* will provide the *best type of information*, and there are no easy answers or shortcut in acquiring these skills. Our students need rehearsal with searching the open web as well as techniques and skills for subscription databases.

Take advantage of the help sections provided by subscription database companies when instructing about advanced search options. Explanations of specific search fields (find all of my search terms or "SmartText Searching,") are helpful to understand and provide additional control over search results. Students need to know the difference if they choose options that expand the search or limit it, such as peer-reviewed, full-text search, or publication type search. EBSCO, as well as others, provides a collection of video and PowerPoint tutorials on the EBSCO help site for each of their products. You can also register for live training sessions or view recorded ones.

CHAPTER 5 | Diving Into The Research Process

One aspect of research that can make an inquiry project feel authentic and credible, but one with which secondary students often struggle, is locating and using primary source documents or interviewing experts. A primary source records the original words of a writer such as a speech, eyewitness account, journal, interview, or autobiography. Librarians can teach techniques on finding primary source documents within databases, the Library of Congress, or the National Archives. Museum collections are now digitally archived and can be unique sources of primary source artifacts, speeches, and documents.

Conducting interviews can also add authenticity to an inquiry topic especially when students discover why the subject is compelling to the interviewee. Encourage students to reach out to established advocacy organizations, special interest groups, and community members who are experts in their fields. Teach students to use social media to locate these members and follow specific hashtags promoted by these organizations. Challenge students to find stakeholders who approach topics from different points of view. Not only will their research be relevant and rewarding, but students may discover aspects of a topic they hadn't considered.

Librarian Stony Evans is a member of the Microsoft Innovative Educator Expert program and uses "Skype in the Classroom" to connect his students with experts in the field. Krystyna, a tenth-grader, presented a demonstration of a robot she built during a virtual Skype-a-thon and Anthony Salacito, vice president of worldwide education at Microsoft, asked her questions. Krystyna was thrilled at the opportunity and reflected, "It made me feel significant and made me realize that distance is no reason not to connect. I am very thankful that they took time to listen to kids around the world and encouraged kids to continue sharing their works with others" (Evans, 2017). A few days after the Skype-a-thon, she had another chance to Skype with a different Microsoft employee, and Krystyna asked questions about qualifications to work at Microsoft. The impact these personal connections made with students will last a lifetime and, as librarian, you can assist in making this happen. More information about Skype in the Classroom can be found at education.microsoft.com/skype-in-the-classroom/overview.

Curating Sources

One of the first things Tiffany Whitehead noticed when moved to a new 6–12 independent school was that the majority of digital resources available were located in various places and were not being well used by the faculty. Whitehead, the upper and middle school librarian at Episcopal School of Baton Rouge, created a public-facing website for her school community and embedded widgets from the online catalog, various databases, and ebooks on the site. She also curated resources for individual classes and linked helpful websites for students. Having a public website can be a valuable advocacy tool to show your community what the students at your school are learning, what resources are available, and how you are involved in the program. It can be a way to promote reading and informational literacy and "brand" your program.

Whether you curate resources on a website, blog, wiki, LibGuides, or page within a LMS like Canvas, Schoology, or Google Classroom, having a dedicated platform where students and teachers know how to access resources and can rely on up-to-date information can prove your credibility with your community. If users find only outdated information and broken links, students won't use the resources and instead slip into bad habits by relying on what is easiest to find. Do you have multiple pathways for students to access library resources? Can students locate and easily find ebooks, databases, or search the library

Online Public Access Catalog (OPAC)? Contact your school's IT department to see if they can provide single sign-on features for easy access. Recruit several secondary students and have them interact with your library site to provide feedback on its ease of use, design, content, usefulness, and overall satisfaction. They are your primary patrons—listen to their advice.

Helpful Hints

Because most secondary schools have digital subscriptions to online databases, librarians need to find ways to help students access the materials and how to remember log-in information and passwords. This list of ideas is recommended by librarians:

> **Create an easy-to-remember URL so students can easily access your library website.** I took the longer URL from my district library entry website www.beaverton.k12.or.us/depts/IT/Library-Resources/Pages/default.aspx and used a URL shortener to create a URL that was easy for my students to remember: bit.ly/sunsetlibrary. Whenever I teach any type of library lesson, I have the students repeat it until they know it. I also print it on posters, bookmarks, and add it to every handout I use. Helpful URL shorteners are: bit.ly, tinyURL, and Google URL Shortener. Some shorteners allow you to customize your URL and others provide a QR code for quick access.
>
> **Build a subject-area resource guide in your LMS and have teachers include it in their course.** I modeled a history subject guide I designed after the type of guides created by academic librarians. The guide details information specifically for history students, such as: where our history books are located in the library, which database subscriptions are used for history, information on primary, secondary, and tertiary

source, information on citing sources, how to access public library databases, and so on. I find that students refer to this guide more often than accessing an external library webpage or site with curated pathfinders because it's located right in their course. Now all history students will receive the same information. A different guide based on a similar template is used for ELA or science classes.

There are several ways to improve student database access (remembering username and password). For example, database companies offer bookmarks that you can customize with your school's user ID and password information. You can provide students with a business card with login information so they can place it in their wallets or encourage them to snap a photo using a phone camera for quick access. Link a shared Google Document with contact information on your school website and then "force a copy" of the document so students have their own version of the library database information in their drive.

Librarians Stony Evans and Kaitlin Price created a HyperDoc (hyperdocs.co) for introducing library resources for an inquiry project for eighth-grade students at Lakeside High School. Having links and brief descriptions of the OPAC and online resources located right on the HyperDoc provided immediate access and directions. Students liked the sense of accomplishment because they could explore the resources independently and work at their own pace. Using a HyperDoc to be an "embedded librarian" during a class project gives us credibility with teachers that we have an expertise worth seeking out. There is a network of teachers who create and freely share their HyperDoc resources with one another. Librarians new to HyperDocs can rework an existing one to get started with this creative, multimedia-driven strategy.

CHAPTER 5 | Diving Into The Research Process

Student Curation Tools

When students search the open web or database subscriptions, they need technology tools to help them organize and sort the information. Curation tools are an important aspect of inquiry-based learning because they give students opportunity to gather, think, evaluate, discard, or save material. Librarians may create pathfinders to direct students to specific sources, while other times, age-appropriate methods for curation tools might be used to save web URLs, images, or share content with others. Many bookmarking tools provide easy-to-use bookmarklets or browser extensions to facilitate clipping articles, pinning images, or bookmarking URLs. The ultimate goal is to have students manage and organize their own research.

What other types of sources should students curate for their inquiry projects? Do students have methods to collect photographs or images? Does their topic lend itself to data visualization? Charts, graphs, and infographics can highlight statistical information in easy-to-read formats. Do students have collection methods for audio recordings, music, or video files, if media formats are needed? If students plan on hyperlinking resources or curating websites to use as sources, how will those be organized? Digital curation is a lifelong skill that is useful beyond the inquiry project.

During an EdWeb webinar on personalized learning, Michelle Luhtala discusses the features of EBSCO Discovery Services (Luhtala, 2017). The way it is set up at her school, all the school databases, digital magazines, MARC records, and state databases are searchable from EBSCO. Students have personal folders to keep track of their search within EBSCO, and database articles and highlighted notes and citations can be sent directly to Google Drive. Many databases companies have powerful tools to create custom searches, set up alerts based on previous searches, and find related articles, videos, audio clips, and other multimedia items. Teaching students to capture the permalinks of these items makes for easier access later. Here are some additional curation tools librarians may want to investigate:

LibGuides (www.springshare.com/libguides/). Numerous academic and secondary librarians use their school's LibGuide (paid subscription) to not only curate sources for specific courses but as a landing page for library information. Librarians can increase the usage of their library's resources and content by featuring them in LibGuides. An excellent feature of LibGuides is the ability to reuse content and share guides with librarians worldwide. Even though my school does not have a subscription to LibGuides, I often direct students to conduct Google Searches using "[topic] LibGuide" because I know academic libraries use this resource for curation and sharing. Students will not have access to that school's academic databases, but the LibGuide will offer other useful web links, multimedia options, or direct patrons to primary source documents related to the topic. This is also a good way to introduce secondary students to college-level library resources.

NoodleTools (www.noodletools.com) is a curation tool (paid subscription) that can save, cite, evaluate sources, organize notes, and outline all of the information for every research project students conduct. Teachers and librarians can track students' progress and provide real-time feedback.

Diigo (www.diigo.com) is a social-bookmarking tool that allows you to curate and tag web content, images, PDFs, and notes. Features like the ability to collaborate with others on curation and annotate webpages make it useful for inquiry learning (free and premium versions).

> Google Keep (keep.google.com) is a free note-taking service that allows students to curate text, lists, images, and audio. Keep notes can be shared with others and easily embedded into other Google products.
>
> **LiveBinders** (www.livebinders.com) curates websites, text, images, and files into an online Binder that can be shared and embedded (free and premium versions).
>
> **SymbalooEd** (www.symbalooedu.com) is a free personalized start page and online visual bookmarking tool that display web content in a creative grid (free and premium versions).

There are too many curation tools to list. Consider these additional options: **Scoop.it**, **Pinterest**, **PearlTrees**, **Evernote**, **Paper.li**, **Flipboard**, and more. A comprehensive list is curated at goo.gl/aXyj8e.

Developing a Researcher's Mindset

For our students to become critical consumers of information, we need to not only help them organize the sources they curate, but help them develop a "researcher's mindset" (Salmons, 2017). Knowing how to think critically, discern fact from opinion, and investigate the reliability and accuracy of information is today an essential literacy. We want our students to be constant evaluators as they read online news, search the internet and database resources, and utilize strategies of critical thinking. It takes time and rehearsal to develop a researcher's mindset. If we want our students to develop new habits of mind, we need instructional strategies that embrace research methods. Consider these statements in Figure 5.1 that reinforce the type of thinking we want our secondary students to embrace.

> **Developing a Researcher's Mindset**
>
> Let's question the foundations of the materials we read and **make a habit of looking for gaps** in the literature.
>
> When we uncover biases, let's use them as the basis for reflection on our own world views and how they might **influence the questions we choose to research.**
>
> Let's think about how to **include global and/or underrepresented perspectives**, including the use of open access or other materials that might not appear in library databases.
>
> Let's brainstorm ways to **reach people who don't typically participate in research.**
>
> Whether we use qualitative or quantitative methods, let's reflect on ways our own backgrounds or prior understandings **influence our interpretation of results.**
>
> Let's reflect on ways to **be transparent about biases** or shortcomings when we report research findings.
>
> Let's consider how to **communicate findings with people outside of academia**—especially those who can put new ideas into practice.

Figure 5.1 Developing a Researcher's Mindset. Adapted with permission from Janet Salmons, Ph.D. from www.methodspace.com/creating-culture-inquiry-classroom/.

These mindset statements have a better chance of being valued and incorporated throughout the inquiry process if students first consider them during the question formulation period. Early in the research process, students should ask, "How are we going to know if the information we seek is credible and relevant? How will we know if the content biased or is missing perspectives?" The ISTE Standards for Students (2016) standard three addresses the need for students to curate a variety of resources and evaluate their accuracy as a knowledge constructor.

ISTE Standard for Students #3: Knowledge Constructor
Students critically curate a variety of resources using digital tools to construct knowledge, produce creative artifacts, and make meaningful learning experiences for themselves and others. Students:

a. Plan and employ effective research strategies to locate information and other resources for their intellectual or creative pursuits.

b. Evaluate the accuracy, perspective, credibility and relevance of information, media, data or other resources.

c. Curate information from digital resources using a variety of tools and methods to create collections of artifacts that demonstrate meaningful connections or conclusions.

d. Build knowledge by actively exploring real-world issues and problems, developing ideas and theories and pursuing answers and solutions.

Credibility Source Investigators

One way I have focused on credibility with students is to make evaluating sources fun by role-playing crime and detective scenarios. Inspired by the popular TV show "CSI: Crime Scene Investigation," I created a HyperDoc (bit.ly/CSIhyperdoc) for my own version of source evaluation: CSI: Credibility Source Investigators (Figure 5.2). Students work in teams to review evidence from news stories and determine if the evidence gathered is accurate and reliable. This activity is an excellent activity to get students diving into source evaluation, especially if the teacher provides some sources that are questionable, sponsored content, or have unreliable images or authors.

Figure 5.2 CSI: Credibility Source Investigators.

Interrogate Your Source

Another activity that can be done any time after students have curated a few sources is to have them work with their inquiry circle and conduct an interrogation of one member's source using the questions on the CRAAP (Currency, Relevance, Authority, Accuracy, and Purpose) Evaluation Worksheet from California State University, Chico (goo.gl/f5E6B8). The worksheet provides interrogation questions for each topic (2010). The activity stimulates creative thinking when students are asked to defend why they are using particular sources.

Here is a role-playing scenario: Interrupt a class work period with an alarm, announcement, a song (e.g., "Mission Impossible" or "Dragnet" theme song), or have the librarian stop by unexpectedly. Announce to your students that this alarm means it's time to "interrogate a research source" from one of your team members. Choose criteria: who is oldest, wearing white socks, closest birthday, and so on. The selected student needs to pick one of their inquiry sources and sit in the "defendant's box." Other team members sit in front of them and play the roles of prosecuting attorney or judge/jury (depending on size of groups). For a few minutes, have the prosecutors "interrogate the source" by asking questions about when the source was updated, how reliable the information is, who sponsored the source, and so on. Students really get into the role-playing aspect and drill their classmates with questions about their sources. Conduct this activity sporadically, and students will get used to defending their sources on the spot. One creative teacher I know steps out of his classroom for a moment and returns wearing a trench coat, detective hat, and notepad. He quickly interrogates several students, then leaves. Students love his creative approach but know he will call them out if their sources are not up to snuff!

Plagiarism

The Purdue Online Writing Lab (2017) defines plagiarism as the "uncredited use (both intentional and unintentional) of somebody else's words or ideas." Secondary students should cite the sources of information used in academic work because citing:

- Makes the work more credible and demonstrates understanding
- Tells the reader where the author found the information
- Allows the reader to learn more, beginning with the listed sources
- Gives credit to the people whose words or ideas are being used
- Protects the writer from plagiarizing

Plagiarism runs rampant in secondary schools. Students, looking for the easy way out, rely on internet searches for easy-to-copy summaries and citations. Other times they panic because they backed themselves into a corner by not leaving enough time to get their work done. They may have difficulty integrating source material into their own writing or even understand the importance of using citations. The more instruction on proper citing and paraphrasing of text, the more students will feel comfortable incorporating expert opinions with their own commentary. Librarians should review the Purdue Online Writing Lab's resources for avoiding plagiarism and make it part of their lessons when conducting inquiry-based research. Another resource worth reviewing is www.plagiarism.org.

In the document "Top Ten Reasons Students Plagiarize and What You Can Do About It" (2012), Michelle Navarre Cleary of DePaul University explains why students copy but also offers advice to educators with strategies and ideas for combatting the issue. A few ideas from Navarre Cleary:

1. Teach students strategies for organizing their notes.

2. Help students learn how to pace and organize their work, especially if the task you have given them is complex and they are novices.

3. Show students examples of student papers with un-cited summaries and paraphrases and require them to identify and correct the problem.

4. Discuss and interrogate with students the values embedded in our practices of citing sources.

5. Make it so hard to plagiarize that they might just as well write the paper. You can do this by requiring documentation of their writing process.

Librarians should also include lessons on copyright and fair use agreements. One idea that resonates with students who are writers, filmmakers, musicians, or artists is to teach students how to grant permissions for their own creative works using Creative Commons licensing (creativecommons.org/licenses). This brings home the idea of copyright and empowers creators to think critically about whether they want their work used for commercial purposes, remixed, or presented for anyone to use with attribution. Teach students to search for "copy friendly" images and always require students to cite their sources. This toolkit is a good place to start: www.smore.com/f677-a-copyright-friendly-toolkit.

Brenda Boyer, a high-school librarian from Kutztown School District, created self-paced lessons in the Canvas LMS platform to measure information literacy skills before seniors begin a capstone research project. Boyer gamified lessons on basic citations, database access, and plagiarism by presenting challenging scenarios, videos to watch, quizzes, and discussion forums where demonstration of proficiency was required to unlock the next level. Digital badges were awarded within the Canvas LMS platform using Badgr (badgr.io) to students who achieved proficiency in using the OPAC, Google searches, evaluating sources, searching databases, and more. What a fun and creative way to ensure basic information literacy skills are reviewed before a major inquiry research project!

Note-Taking Strategies

Note-taking techniques not only assist students with accurate and relevant notes but also reinforce using proper citations and avoiding plagiarism. Students rely too heavily on quotations in academic writing and often do not add their own commentary or insights. Digital sources tempt students to copy and paste large sections without proper in-text citations or discussion of the cited text. Secondary students who are conducting research for an academic paper need direct instruction on the uses of, and distinctions among, original quotes, paraphrases, and summaries. Note-taking strategies can assist students with identifying quotations and paraphrases, but the real benefit is they require the student to pause and re-read their sources carefully and deliberately. Note-taking strategies vary depending on the age and complexity of the research.

Bruce Ballenger, author of the *The Curious Researcher: A Guide to Writing Research Papers* (2012) offers some note-taking strategies to help students synthesize the information they read. When using the double-entry journal (sometimes known as a T-Chart) students divide a paper into two columns and write down the bibliographic information for the source in one column, including a compilation of quotes, paraphrases, and summaries (see Table 5.1). After careful examination of the material, the student responds with a "fastwrite" in the second column with their own interpretations, feelings, additional questions, and thoughts. Some students even hide the left column so the commentary is original and authentic and they aren't tempted to copy.

Ballinger also recommends the research log as an alternative way to take notes from sources. Students keep a running log of all sources reviewed and consulted. Once again, the bibliographic information is documented. The first entry is an open-ended fastwrite using the heading "What Strikes Me Most." Next, the student adds information under "Source Notes" (quotes, paraphrases, etc.). "The Source Reconsidered" is the final entry, where the student goes back and takes a more focused look at the original quotes and considers new ideas. Both of these methods encourage thoughtful commentary while asking students to consider how the quote or summary supports their main idea or thesis.

Table 5.1 Double-Entry Journal

Original Source:

Singer, P. & Mason, J. (2006). *The way we eat: why our food choices matter.* Rodale.

Direct Quotes, Paraphrases, and Summaries	"Fastwrite" Commentary/Response
"Almost all chickens sold in supermarkets—known in the industry as 'broilers'—are raised in very large sheds. A typical shed measures 490 feet long by 45 feet wide and will hold 30,000 or more chickens" (pg. 23).	Why should we care that chickens grown in captivity fill a room with no room to move? Farming culture promotes overstocking in a typical 490x45 foot shed and is used in today's factory-farm production to raise large numbers of poultry while maintaining costs. As consumers, do we need to be concerned about the ethical treatment of animals if it hits us in the pocketbook? These are interesting questions to explore in my essay.

NoodleTools, as mentioned previously, is a paid subscription that provides a digital platform for students to take notes from their sources. Sources are automatically linked when adding information to Notecards. Space is provided for students to copy a direct quotation from a source; there is a paraphrase or summary section for students to explain quotes in their own words, and a section called "My Ideas" where students do original thinking and write how information fits with what they already know or what additional questions arise. A place to tag the notecard with a category is available, as is a place to document the URL, page numbers, and other useful things (see Figure 5.3). The benefit of using a digital tool like NoodleTools is that it emphasizes the original thinking during the reading and re-reading of the source. Teachers and librarians can also track student progress.

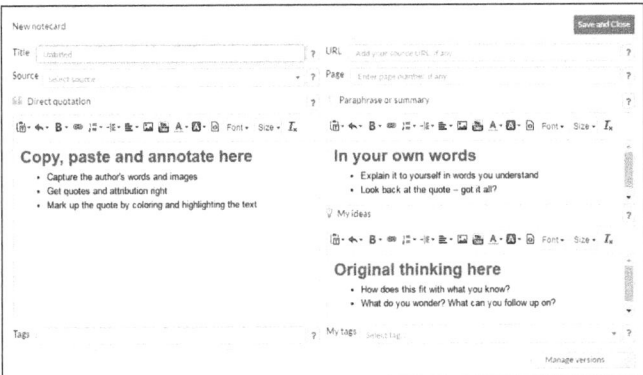

Figure 5.3 NoodleTools, Used for Note-Taking. Used with permission.

Google Forms

I created "digital notecards" using a Google Form for an English literary analysis assignment. The form identified the source/author, the type of source, presented a space to add categories, direct quotes, commentary, and citation information. Students filled out their own form for every "notecard" (see Figure 5.4). The information populated a spreadsheet that was shared with the teacher and librarian. Tracking progress was easy because the teacher or librarian could provide feedback about quality of sources or commentary. The student could also sort the sort the notecards by category, which was very helpful in determining if their research was balanced or if they needed additional sources to support a claim.

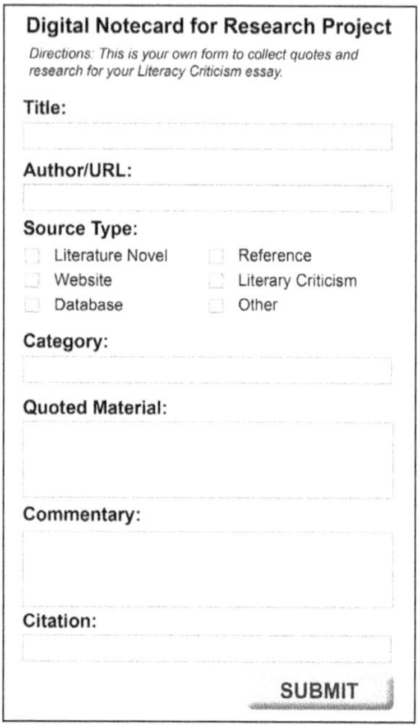

Digital Notecard for Research Project

Directions: This is your own form to collect quotes and research for your Literacy Criticism essay.

Title:

Author/URL:

Source Type:

- Literature Novel
- Website
- Database
- Reference
- Literary Criticism
- Other

Category:

Quoted Material:

Commentary:

Citation:

SUBMIT

Figure 5.4 Using Google Forms as a Digital Notecard.

It doesn't matter which platform is used for note-taking. What is important is that students are asked to provide evidence and offer interpretations, so the thoughts and words in their own work are coming from the deep thinking the sources provide. It does, however, take time and explicit instruction in the how and why we take notes, and how to incorporate quotes into academic writing. The librarian can suggest different note-taking approaches, visual-thinking strategies, and emphasize the importance of processing time so our students aren't tempted to use another's ideas as their own.

Ebooks for Beginner Researchers

During the summer of 2015, required reading for all the incoming sixth-graders from Central Middle School was the novel *Wonder* (2015) by R.J. Palacio. Teachers schoolwide used the story and themes from the book as an anchor text for beginning-of-the-year activities. In the novel, the main character participates in an ancient Egypt project, so teacher-librarian Tiffany Whitehead collaborated with sixth-grade ELA/SS teachers to borrow the Egyptian theme to teach their students how to conduct research.

These new middle-school students were not familiar with using ebooks for research, so Whitehead introduced several ancient Egypt reference ebooks. Students began with a scavenger hunt activity to identify key elements of the ebook (see Figure 5.5).

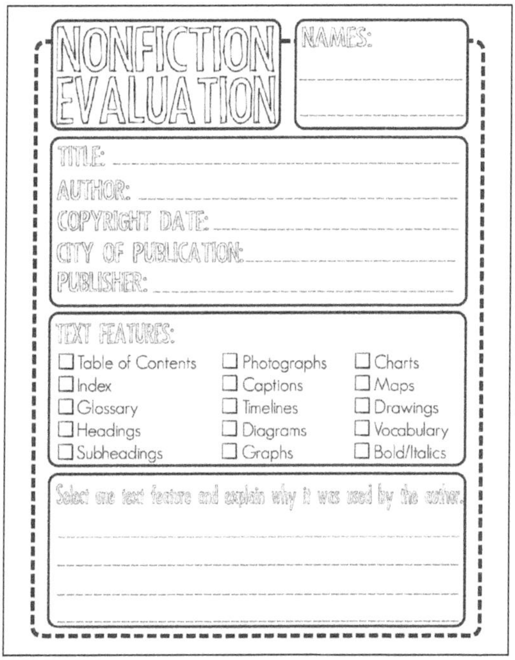

NONFICTION EVALUATION

NAMES:

TITLE:

AUTHOR:

COPYRIGHT DATE:

CITY OF PUBLICATION:

PUBLISHER:

TEXT FEATURES:

- ☐ Table of Contents
- ☐ Index
- ☐ Glossary
- ☐ Headings
- ☐ Subheadings
- ☐ Photographs
- ☐ Captions
- ☐ Timelines
- ☐ Diagrams
- ☐ Graphs
- ☐ Charts
- ☐ Maps
- ☐ Drawings
- ☐ Vocabulary
- ☐ Bold/Italics

Select one text feature and explain why it was used by the author.

Figure 5.5 Ebook Scavenger Hunt.

This activity allowed students to connect what they already knew about print books and apply that knowledge to ebook materials. Students soon realized not all ebooks are formatted the same as their print counterparts. Multi-user ebooks are excellent for beginning research instruction because everyone can access and analyze the digital content at the same time.

Providing direct instruction in how to establish a research question and take notes is critical for young researchers. During structured inquiry lessons, Whitehead and the teachers guided students through the process of selecting a topic, identifying keywords, writing a research question, and brainstorming. Students learned how create a citation and how to copy down a direct quote from the eBook. Once notes were taken from the sources, sentence starters were provided to assist the sixth-graders in outlining the material, which included instructions and definitions of key terms such as *thesis, transitions,* and *supporting evidence*. Students went on to prepare a visual presentation that coordinated with their writing and was shared at a family and community event. This story illustrates the various degrees of teacher instruction and intervention needed to help students be successful. When planning, consider what type of age-appropriate structures will be needed for all learners.

Differentiation

Students conduct research to share what they know, but also to extend the conversation and examine viewpoints from various lenses. Not all inquiry leads to an academic paper as there are many creative formats for publishing student research that may be more appropriate for certain individuals (see Chapter 6). Special populations may need additional strategies during the gathering and reading of sources, as well as note-taking and summarizing of research. Librarians can personalize inquiry instruction by working with teachers to identify students who need assistance and provide one-on-one instruction.

Most online database companies offer text-to-speech capabilities within their software. Students can listen with headphones and follow along as the software reads the source information. This can assist with word recognition, pronunciation skills, and build fluency. Translation options within databases provide ELLs the opportunity to read content in their native language to assist with comprehension. Tools such as Google's Read and Write for Chrome (free and paid versions) provide support tools that can scan and read documents, websites, and PDFs. Librarians can add basic captions to simplified tutorial screencasts so students can review instructions by video.

A career and college readiness program called AVID (Advancement Via Individual Determination) recommends that educators provide ELLs with scaffolds and strategies for reading, writing, and speaking to make the content relevant and accessible for a variety of language levels (2017). These students need to build background knowledge to understand the context of the material and make connections with their own understanding. Pre-teaching vocabulary words and concepts before the student reads is encouraged because the text complexity can be challenging and affects interpretation. Consider providing students with inquiry text sets, but require the learners to locate one source by following a step-by-step protocol. Teach students "text-marking" strategies as they read content information to focus their comprehension and understanding. After an initial read, suggest that students write questions or comments in the margins to summarize the material. Once the source material is read, utilize sentence frames for writing and/or discussion activities. To differentiate the learning for various abilities, educators need to plan tasks that have multiple entry points so students' work can be adjusted to meet individualized learning needs.

Sentence Frames

By using differentiated sentence frames with varying levels of complexity, students can offer more sophisticated responses. IB history teacher Alisa Harvey weaves "explicit language instruction" into her history lessons using techniques from "About Constructing Meaning" (E.L. Achieve, 2016). She combines these techniques with the OPCVL framework analyzing historical documents. This scaffolding can be in the form of sentence frames or paragraphs. Harvey shared, "My colleagues and I created OPCVL sentence starters to help students talk about and document their observations using academic language. The frames are helpful because they focus on the content knowledge and students are not hindered by language construction." Below are two different examples to assist history students with source evaluations.

> **O**rigin: This source _____ was written by _____ in _____. The author _____.
>
> **P**urpose: Based on *(evidence)* _____ this document was created to _____ *(Persuade, Inform, Debate, Convince, Detail, Outline, Communicate, Describe, Entice, Sell)* so that _____. The original audience was _____.
>
> **C**ontent: The document contains _____ and includes details about _____.
>
> **V**alue: This source is valuable for historians trying to understand _____ because _____.
>
> **L**imitations: However, a limitation of this source is _____.

OPCVL Paragraph

This source (*title*) was written by (*author*) in (*date and location*). The author was (*Who is this person?*). Based on (*evidence*), this document was created to (*see keywords*) so that (*intended outcome*). The original audience was (*who*). The document contains _____ and includes details about _____. This source is valuable for historians trying to understand (*restate question*) because (*evaluate the origin/purpose/content*) and because (*evaluate the origin/purpose/content*). However, a limitation is (*evaluate origin/purpose/content*). Another limitation is (*evaluate origin/purpose/content*).

Paragraph Summary with Source Integration

Personalized instruction may require the librarian to help struggling students synthesize information from their sources. Provide students with different colored highlighters for text marking. Select one color and have the student highlight the title, author, and date of publication. Choose another color to summarize main ideas of each topic from their notes, another to locate evidence in those paragraphs, summaries, and so on. Color-code the provided paragraph summary plan below. The text marking and color highlights might be enough to get students started on their writing.

"Title of article," by Author(s), is an article about/that *(state authors' claim, purpose, or main idea)*. First, the authors *(present tense verb) (summarize first main idea from reading)*. _____ *Give an example from reading to support your idea* _____. This example shows/emphasizes *(explain how example supports main idea)*. Second/Also/Additionally, they *(present tense verb) (summarize second main idea from reading)*. _____*Give an example from reading to support your idea*_____. This is important/significant because *(explain importance)*. Finally/Lastly, Author's Name *(present tense verb) (summarize last main idea from reading)*. *Give an example from the reading to support your idea* *(explain how your example supports the author's idea)*. Overall/Generally/In conclusion, the authors *(present tense verb) (final concluding message from the reading)*.

Sentence frames can also be helpful question prompts for librarians as they are working with students one-on-one. Providing a comprehensive word bank builds students vocabulary skills and adds sophistication and depth to their writing. While it is not the primary role of the librarian to conduct individual tutoring for special needs populations, knowing and using these strategies will benefit students you encounter.

In the Spotlight

Media Literacy

Common Sense Media defines media literacy as "the ability to access, analyze, evaluate, create, and communicate using information in all forms" (Daunic, 2017). Media literacy empowers people to be critical thinkers and makers, effective communicators, and active citizens. Since secondary students use current media in their inquiry learning, librarians should be familiar with their advantages and pitfalls. This relevant topic is so vast that it lends itself to its own book (see recommended reading in Appendix B) but the following are resources to help school librarians with their own understanding, developing fact-checking habits of mind during inquiry projects, curriculum ideas, and web resources.

In a blog post written for School Library Journal, "Truth, Truthiness, Triangulation: A News Literacy Toolkit for a 'Post-Truth' World" (2016), Joyce Valenza discusses the need to teach news literacy across all disciplines. Citing the Stanford Graduate School of Education report, *Evaluating Information: The Cornerstone of Civic Online Reasoning* (Wineburg, McGrew, Breakstone & Ortega, 2016), Valenza sees a need to build lessons to assist students in discerning the flood of news media, but also introduce the notion of "triangulation" and validating data and information from more than two news sources. The blog post goes on to define "truthiness" and "fake news" and provide practical ideas for evaluating sources, vocabulary for discussing creditability, and resources for a "post-truth" teaching toolkit.

Valenza includes an excellent resource: *False, Misleading, Clickbait-y, and Satirical "News" Sources* (goo.gl/YpLlFu) from Melissa Zimzars, assistant professor of communication and media at Merrimack College. Zimsars lists over 1,000 website URLs that have been categorized using the following tags: extreme bias, fake news, conspiracy, unreliable, satire, hate news, political, rumor mill, state news, clickbait, junk science, proceed with caution, credible, or unknown. Valenza's blog post is a must-read for every secondary librarian. Show your students the examples from The Verification Handbook's *Educator's Guide: Types of Online Fakes* (verificationhandbook.com/additionalmaterial/types-of-online-fakes.php) to teach them about the different categories of online hoaxes and fakes: real photos from unrelated events; art, ads, film and staged scenes; photoshopped images; fake accounts; altered manual retweets; fake tweets; and fake websites.

I recommend librarians subscribe to *The Sift*, a weekly newsletter curated by former journalist Peter D. Adams of the News Literacy Project (2017). Its goals are to teach students how to "differentiate information that is presented fairly, accurately and contextually from opinion, rumor and disinformation." This weekly newsletter provides an overview of the current-events issues of the week and has helped me to stay up-to-date with the constantly changing 24/7 news cycle. Adams provides commentary on breaking news, links to the source news articles, classroom discussion ideas, and action ideas. I appreciate the examples of viral rumors and facts versus fake news; I often share these articles with students. The News Literacy Project has also launched a virtual classroom program called Checkology (thenewsliteracyproject.org/services/checkology) where students can discover how to effectively navigate today's news landscape by mastering core skills and concepts.

Get your whole school involved with media literacy by promoting and organizing activities every November for Media Literacy Week (medialiteracyweek.us) sponsored by the National Association of Media Literacy Education (NAMLE). The NAMLE website (namle.net) is a wealth of information with resources to support Common Core State Standards, publications for parents, codes of best practices in fair use for media literacy education, the NAMLE annual conference, and more.

In 2017, the Young Adult Library Services Association (YALSA), a subspecialty of the American Library Association, published a *Teen Literacies Toolkit* that uses the "fake news" phenomenon as an approach to print and digital literacies. YALSA reexamines and discusses culturally inclusive print and digital literacy strategies to assist teens in making sense of their world. Helpful sections on recognizing a teen's cultural context and understanding today's media environment are valuable resources for school librarians. Advice such as fact checking a story with another type of news resource (Snopes.com, Politifact.com, or the *Washington Post*'s Fact

Checker column) are shared as well as explanations of Google search algorithms and vocabulary terms. Share this 32-page document with your entire staff and make sure to review its extensive recommended resource section.

Other excellent media literacy sources include:

Common Sense Media News and Media Literacy Toolkit (www.commonsense.org /education/toolkit/ news-and-media-literacy) contains lesson plans, activities, and videos for students K–12. This can be a starting point for conversations with parents or teachers who are looking for activities with teens.

The Verification Handbook (verificationhandbook.com) provides the tools, techniques, and step-by-step guidelines for how to deal with user-generated content during emergencies.

Hoax-Slayer (www.hoax-slayer.net) debunks email and social media hoaxes, thwarts internet scammers, combats spam, and educates web users about email, social media, and internet security issues.

Our task is huge. Media literacy requires a different mindset and critical thinking about the messages we receive and create. We want our students to "be informed, reflective, and engaged participants in a democratic society." As educators, we have an obligation to knock down walls of confirmation bias that entrenches thinking within a bubble. Our society won't move forward if we don't encourage our students to think objectively. Media literacy education should be embedded in inquiry-based lessons when appropriate, so all students can identify, understand, and create their own meanings from media messages (National Association for Media Literacy Education, 2007).

CHAPTER 6

Publishing and Performance Tasks

The novel *The Things They Carried* (1990) by Tim O'Brien inspired Westlake High School students to learn more about the Vietnam War and the men and women who sacrificed their lives for our country. Each year, English III AP students research a person whose name appears on the Vietnam Veterans Memorial Wall; they create a video presentation honoring the individual's life and the time in which they lived. If possible, the student contacts the family and, using primary source images and interviews, creates a video tribute to the veteran. Teacher-librarian Carolyn Foote reports this has been an ongoing project of the English III AP classes at Westlake for many years. To date, there are over 1,800 videos housed on their website (virtualvietnam.eanesisd.net), honoring the servicemen and women who gave their lives in Vietnam. The story of *The Things They Carried* becomes relevant for the student producers as they begin to understand the complexity of this historical event.

Authentic Audience

We ask our students to engage in research not only to learn something, but to share it and make a difference. It is powerful for students to honor real people by telling their stories. The fact that the virtual Vietnam project has been ongoing for years says something about the importance of the project to the Westlake community. Various oral, written, graphic, and multimedia formats provide students creative outlets to reach an audience when they have an important message. When presenting, students need to thoughtfully consider the following (Ophea, 2016):

- The genre for presenting information (e.g., oral, visual, written, multimedia, performance).

- The target audience (e.g., audience, peers, teammate, younger students, educator, family, community member).

- The purpose or goal (e.g., to inform, persuade, instruct, refute, or promote).

English teacher Rebecca Larson encourages using a variety of writing styles when conducting inquiry-based lessons. While she spends a great deal of time teaching students the information research process, she also encourages students to write persuasively, with narrative or expository techniques. When students are empowered to choose the audience and the type of publication—whether digital or written—they begin to realize the power of their voice, and understand they can educate or influence others. Too often, we rob our students of this experience because, 99% of the time, students submit work for only the teacher's eyes. During the inquiry process, our students should be asking, "So what? Why is it important for others to learn and know about _____?" We send a strong message to our students when we provide an authentic context for sharing their learning—no matter the format. With an authentic audience, students are "driven by the knowledge that their writing will leave the school, go out into the world, and be judged not for their ability to respond to an assignment, but for their ability to reach other people through their writing" (Fenton, 2016).

Some teachers are hesitant to conduct authentic inquiry projects because it feels overwhelming to do all the planning and organizing up front. This is where librarians can step in as co-teachers. If a student is passionate about their topic and feels like they have something to say, they should feel empowered to seek out their own audience. Oftentimes we need to nudge them and ask, "Who would benefit from knowing what you have learned from your investigation? What is the best format for delivering your message?" Let the student decide. Another peer group is always an excellent option for an audience. Or, if they interviewed someone for their inquiry project, ask the interviewee to visit the classroom and hear the student share their research. Having a few people who are invested in the topic can be a more effective audience than planning for a whole auditorium—which, honestly, can feel overwhelming for both students and teachers alike. Invite parents to sit on a panel for design-thinking presentations, or encourage students to report findings to community organizations. Consider hosting a TEDx-style evening where students speak about their inquiry-based projects, or feature a film festival showcase of video projects. If student work isn't getting to the right audience or out into the community, students, librarians, and teachers should reflect how they could make this happen in the future.

Online Communities

Joining an online community that is already conducting collaborative projects is another way to have a built-in audience. Many of these communities connect classrooms for inquiry projects, or celebrate the learning in a public forum. Spend some time reviewing these options as well as the online news magazines shared in Chapter 3.

> **TED-Ed Clubs** (ed.ted.com/clubs) supports students in discovering, exploring, and presenting their big ideas in the form of short, TED-style talks.
>
>> Read "What Students Can Learn from Giving TEDx Talks" (ww2.kqed.org/mindshift/2014/11/25/what-students-can-learn-from-giving-tedx-talks)
>>
>> Visit "The TEDxClassroomProject" (tedxproject.wordpress.com)
>
> **Youth Voices** (www.youthvoices.live) encourages students to read and write blog posts about their own passions, connect with other students, comment on each other's work, and create multimedia posts for each other.
>
> **ePals Classroom Exchange** (www.epals.com) is an online platform where teachers and students from around the world connect, communicate, and collaborate.
>
> **Web-Based Inquire Science Environment** (WISE) (wise.berkeley.edu) is a research-based platform that fosters exploration and science inquiry, and encourages students to participate in real science data collection.
>
> **Your Commonwealth** (www.yourcommonwealth.org) is a website created and crafted by young people, students, and emerging youth leaders from Africa, Asia, the Caribbean and

Americas, Europe, and the Pacific. Students may gain new perspectives by joining a project outside their country.

Publishing Options

Below is a list of more than 100 ways students can demonstrate their learning and publish to an authentic audience. Each idea has a unique audience and purpose, so have students justify why the format is appropriate or effective in delivering the message for their chosen audience.

Academic Journal	Chart
Advertisement	Children's Book
Almanac	Classified Ad
Animation	Collected Works
Annotated Bibliography	Concept Map
Annual Report	Comic Book
Art Collection	Commercial
Atlas	Community Event
Audiobook	Comparative Study
Augmented Reality Tour	Clinical Study
Autobiography	Cultural Experience
Biography	Diary
Blog	Debate
Brochure	Dictionary
Book	Discussion Forum
Calendar	Documentary
Cartoon	Ebook
Catalog	Editorial

Encyclopedia
Essay
Eulogy
Exhibition
FAQ
Film Festival
Flyer
Government Publication
Grant
Graphic Novel
Guide Book
Historical Newspaper
How-to Guide
Infographic
Infomercial
Instructional Film
Interactive Map
Interview
Journal
Lab Manual
Lecture
Letter to ... (Editor, Community Leaders, President, Author)
Lesson
Lyrics
Magazine
Map

Marketing Campaign
Memoir
Movie
Museum Collection
Music Video
Myth
Newscast
Newspaper
Oral Tradition
Pamphlet
Peer-Reviewed Journal
Photo journal
Picture Book
Play
Podcast
Poem
Poster
Presentation
Promotional Video
Proposal
PSA (Public Service Announcement)
Quiz
Radio Program
Realia
Report
Research Paper

CHAPTER 6 | Publishing and Performance Tasks

Resource Guide	Stop Motion Video
Resume	Storyboard
Review	Study Guide
Scrapbook	Tabloid News
Script	Television Show
"Shark Tank" Pitch	Textbook
Sermon	Time Capsule
Short Story	Timeline
Silent Film	Travel Guide
Simulation	Tutorial
Song	Website
Speaker Series	Webinar
Speech	Workshop
Spoken Word Poetry	Virtual Reality Experience
Step-by-Step Instructions	Zine

Standards

Both the AASL National School Library Standards (2018) and Common Core State Standards address the value of establishing a real audience for students. The English Language Arts Standards (2017) ask students to "produce clear and coherent writing in which the development and organization are appropriate to task, purpose, and audience." The Common Core also expects students to write for "a range of discipline-specific tasks, purposes, and audiences." The ISTE Standards for Students (2016) also address choosing appropriate platforms to meet the goals of the communicator.

ISTE Standard for Students #6: Creative Communicator
Students communicate clearly and express themselves creatively for a variety of purposes using the platforms, tools, styles, formats, and digital media appropriate to their goals. Students:

a. Choose the appropriate platforms and tools for meeting the desired objectives of their creation or communication.

b. Create original works or responsibly repurpose or remix digital resources into new creations.

c. Communicate complex ideas clearly and effectively by creating or using a variety of digital objects such as visualizations, models, or simulations.

d. Publish or present content that customizes the message and medium for their intended audiences.

A "variety of digital objects" can provide different types of platforms appropriate for inquiry-based projects. Oftentimes, students are more engaged because the technology tools assist them in creating a more professional-looking project, or provide them the means to communicate to a larger audience through publishing.

In my high-school library, we created the Apollo Press Student Publishing Center (see Figure 6.1) as a place where students have access to digital tools for creative class projects and publications. Students have access to a color printer, bookbinding machine, and creative supplies for bookmaking. In addition to written platforms, students can use the green screen to make professional looking videos or stop-motion videos. We provide microphones for podcasting and even have a 3D printer to design original pieces. Teachers are more willing to try publishing projects because they know I am there to encourage

CHAPTER 6 | Publishing and Performance Tasks

and assist the students with their creative works. The publishing center is now expanding to include self-published books and zines in our library collection, and it showcases digital projects on a library TV.

Figure 6.1 Apollo Press Student Publishing Center.

Inspiring Stories of Publishing and Sharing

Student research can be presented using a variety formats depending on the goals of the assignment. There is power when students intentionally choose a particular format because they know it will have the greatest impact on their intended audience. The following stories showcase creative ways librarians and teachers provide real-world experiences where students can demonstate their learning.

CNN News Panel

Librarian Carolyn Foote shares a creative way sophomores at Westlake High School reported their research from an English/language arts class. The students investigated current-events topics, so their teacher organized a simulated CNN News panel presentation. Students with comparable topics sat together on the panel and discussed their research. A moderator asked clarifying questions and kept the conversation going. To keep the audience engaged during the panel presentations, the rest of the class participated in a "back channel" discussion using Today's Meet (todaysmeet.com). During the back channel, students commented on the panel discussion and offered their own opinions. This is an excellent way to get everyone involved and engaged.

Published Book and Traveling Exhibit

Ninth grade humanities students from Roosevelt High School, in Portland, Oregon, were recognized for their Freedom Fighter Project. The Roosevelt "Rough Writers" interviewed civil rights and community leaders to capture personal testimonies and insight about civil rights. The students learned how these leaders worked to advance the civil rights of various races, cultures, and religions in Portland, and they published a book of essays. Along with assistance from the Oregon Historical Society and college students from a local university, the ninth-graders created the Freedom Fighters traveling exhibit. This visual exhibit of quotes and images traveled to numerous sites in the community, such as churches, colleges, and government offices. There are so many key areas a librarian could be involved in this project.

CHAPTER 6 | Publishing and Performance Tasks

Civics Class Debate

Following the format of televised presidential debates, librarian Stony Evans hosted the ninth grade social studies debate at Lakeside High School. The goal was for students to improve skills in critical and analytical thinking, and social and oral communications, through multifaceted research. Civics classes chose three current-event topics and began their research using EBSCO and Opposing Viewpoints databases. Evans reported there was total student-to-student engagement in small group- and whole-class planning in preparation for the big day. Debaters were elected by each of the classes, and nondebaters were given an evaluation form to complete during the presentations. Administrators and school board members were invited to be guest moderators. Post-debate discussions, alongside written reflections, followed the official results of the debate.

Blogging to Make a Difference

I was teaching a digital citizenship unit with an eighth grade class and wanted them to have an authentic experience of using technology to make a difference. The class brainstormed ideas of how eighth-graders could change or affect people's behaviors. They settled on the topic of environmental impact and studied ways to influence or educate the community. Students decided to start a blog after being inspired by a TakingITGlobal 40-day challenge. The students planned their own forty-day blog challenge, and we discussed the proper protocol for writing on a blog platform and how to protect their privacy. After spending several weeks researching their topics, group members wrote blog posts and collaborated with teammates about messaging and design. Each day, two students posted a message on our "Tread Lightly" blog about how to be a good steward of the environment by recycling, reducing emissions, using less packaging, planting trees, and so on. Blog posts educated the reader, encouraged action, offered tips and resources, and inspired the community to care. Students learned the power of social media when I signed up our class to receive #Comments4Kids. The excitement of comments on our blog increased the motivation to research and write because students knew someone was reading their blog and cared enough about the topic to comment.

 In the Spotlight

Technology Tools for Publishing

Finding avenues for students to publish and share their inquiry research with the larger community celebrates their hard work and creates a lasting archive of their accomplishments. If students create an EPUB of their written inquiry project, it can be downloaded and read on various handheld devices. Here are a few ways to publish written work:

> **Issuu** (issuu.com). Offers a free version where students can create an embeddable online magazine.
>
> **Book Creator** (bookcreator.com). Create ebooks to be read on iPad, Android, and Windows tablets. Create a book and publish it to Apple's iBooks Store.
>
> **On Demand Books** (www.ondemandbooks.com). Publish student research as a paperback book using the Espresso Book Machine.
>
> Infographics: Represent information using a visual or graphics format using **Piktochart** (piktochart.com), **Canva** (www.canva.com/create/infographics), or **Venngage** (venngage.com).

Publishing to the web is very effective because it is simple and can include images and multimedia options. Blogs are more interactive than static websites, but be sure to include lessons on appropriate digital citizenship to protect student privacy.

> **EduBlogs** (edublogs.org). A blogging platform for blogs, e-portfolios, and websites (Free for students; Pro).
>
> **Kidblog** (kidblog.org/home). Provides K–12 teachers with tools to safely publish student writing (Premium).
>
> **Google Sites** (sites.google.com). Free and easy way to create and share webpages.

Presentation tools leverage students' visual and multimedia options, and most are embeddable on the web.

> **PowerPoint, Keynote, and Google Slides.** Traditional options for student slide deck presentations.
>
> **Adobe Spark** (spark.adobe.com). Create video stories, webpages, and graphics with user-friendly online software.
>
> **TouchCast Studio** (www.touchcast.com/studio). Use green screen technology to create creative video productions

Screencasting tools provide teachers and students the ability to record presentations from their computer screen or during presentations.

> **Screencastify** (www.screencastify.com). Capture, edit, and share screencasts easily; works on Chromebooks.
>
> **Screencast-O-Matic** (screencast-o-matic.com). Create and share screen recordings.
>
> **Microsoft PowerPoint** with **Office Mix** screen recording (mix.office.com). Creates screencast videos within PowerPoint slides.

Quicktime Player v10 (support.apple.com/en-us/ HT201066). Offers video and screen capturing options.

Online interactions provide opportunities for students to share inquiry projects at a distance.

Google Hangouts (hangouts.google.com). Web conferencing and screen-sharing capabilities.

Skype (www.skype.com/en). Video web conference software for online sharing.

Today's Meet (todaysmeet.com). Discussion software that allows participants to backchannel during presentations.

CHAPTER 7

Assessment and Inquiry Tools

A 10th-grade social studies teacher approaches you and asks if you could assist her students, who are struggling with research. She wants you to evaluate their sources and give feedback on the students' bibliographies. Can you help? Librarian Michelle Luhtala tackled this scenario by creating a system that personalizes feedback for the students at New Canaan High School. Luhtala first created a series of modules in Moodle (LMS) that requires students to complete lessons on how to cite using the MLA8 guidelines. This review clears some confusion, but if students still want assistance or just want her to look over their work, they can submit their bibliographies to Luhtala for review. Using a Google form, students submit a link to a Google Document containing their working bibliography. All student requests populate a spreadsheet in which Luhtala evaluates the works cited. Using a Document with a comprehensive list of comments (goo.gl/asdZZo) to provide observations about the page formatting, the type of sources, citation errors, and MLA formatting, Luhtala gives feedback by listing numbers correlating to each comment/error (e.g., StudentName 1, 14, 26).

COMMENT LIST EXAMPLES

1. Page Format
- Center the header;
- Set page margins to 1";
- Hanging margins (.5");
- Use 12-point Times New Roman font, double-spaced;
- Do not skip lines between citations;
- Alphabetized citations.
- For annotated bibliography, check sample on MLA 8 page.

14. Author (element 1)
- Sequence: Last name first, first name last. [for one]; Last name first, first name last, and firstnamefirst lastnamelast. [for two]; Always place middle names or their initials after first name (e.g., Mellencamp, John C.)

26. Research
- Reference: You have too many encyclopedic resources in this bibliography.

Students receive an autoreply email with the feedback, which includes links to documents where they can learn about their mistakes and review proper MLA/APA guidelines. Not only do her comments provide personalized feedback for every student, but the collected data is evaluated by the librarian and teachers to determine where future instruction is needed. A slide deck of the top 10 mistakes is shared so everyone can benefit. Examples from real student work (without student names) illustrate common errors.

This is a wonderful way for the librarian to support student learning and help students critically evaluate the types of sources they are using in their research. This type of formative assessment comes at a critical point during the inquiry process, and students are more willing to look for errors or find additional resources because the feedback is given during a time when they are still growing and learning. Luhtala shared that this process has gone through several iterations before she settled on the final form and email feedback. How can you provide personalized learning in your library setting?

Formative Assessment

The primary goal of assessment during the inquiry process is to impact student learning. A range of formative and summative assessments is utilized to provide targeted information and evaluation of student work. Formative assessments generally are not graded and are used to provide feedback or as an ongoing diagnostic tool. To be effective, they should occur frequently and be shared with students in a timely manner, so students can redirect efforts or clarify instruction. Students may need direct instruction in how to effectively use inquiry tools, and learners should be involved in creating criteria for rubrics. Provide students with strategies and opportunities to assess their own learning as well as give appropriate feedback to peers. The entire formative and summative assessment process should be reviewed by both the librarian and teacher to ensure it is aligned with learning targets.

Guided Inquiry Design by Kuhlthau, Maniotes, and Caspari (2012) provides different types of inquiry tools based on the situation. The use of these inquiry tools should constantly be shifted and evaluated based on what the students have previously learned, or what type of intervention is required. Table 7.1 clarifies how guided inquiry design uses the strategies of the six Cs from Kuhlthau's information search process.

Inquiry journals are an example of a formative assessment that provides students with an opportunity to document thinking around their research questions. Initially, the journal could be used for jotting down ideas from sources of information; they might include lists of questions, facts, or ideas that occur to the students as they work through their initial readings. The journal continues to be used for conversations during inquiry circles and can help students make decisions about questions for investigations or summaries after in-depth reading of sources. Students use the journal to recall, summarize, paraphrase, and rehearse how to complete in-text citations. The teacher can leave comments and suggestions to deepen student's thinking. Students begin to see the research as a process rather than a means to an end goal of a paper or project.

Table 7.1 Inquiry Tools

INQUIRY TOOLS
GUIDED INQUIRY DESIGN

Inquiry Tools	Strategies	Embedded Strategies for Inquiry
Inquiry Communities	Collaborating	An inquiry community is a collaborative environment where students learn with each other in a large group.
Inquiry Circles	Conversing	Inquiry circles are small groups organized for conversations about interesting ideas, meaningful questions, and emerging insights.
Inquiry Journals	Composing	Inquiry journals are a routine structure in guided inquiry. In journals, students compose independent reflections and construct new meaning throughout the inquiry process. Students complete tasks in the journal to bring to the inquiry circle collaborations and discussions.
Inquiry Logs	Choosing	Inquiry logs provide a way for keeping track of quality sources that are selected for addressing an inquiry question. Logs track student decision making through the process.
Inquiry Charts	Charting	Inquiry charts enable visualizing ideas and organizing to make decisions, synthesize ideas, and create in the inquiry process.
Inquiry Tools	Continuing	All of the inquiry tools are used for continuing and sustaining the inquiry process to completion.

Source: Used with permission from Kuhithau, C., Maniotes, L., Caspari, A. (2012). *Guided Inquiry Design: A Framework for Inquiry in Your School.* Libraries Unlimited; Westport, CT.

Possible journal prompts:

- What are your successes thus far?
- Write about something that surprised you or was new to you.
- Write something that you already know about. Tell how you know.
- List ideas that you want to know more about.
- What questions or concerns about the project did you have before the meeting? In what way(s) were these questions answered?
- What questions or concerns are still unanswered?
- Describe the connection that you are making between your background information and the application of your research question.

Offering students various methods to demonstrate what they've learned throughout the inquiry process cements their own learning, and it provides insight into students' thinking. Ontario Ministry of Education (2010) suggest librarians and teachers can use a variety of observations, strategies, and tools, such as:

- Formal and informal observations
- Discussions, learning conversations, questioning, student-led conferences
- Tasks done in groups, inquiry-circle evaluations
- Demonstrations, performances
- Projects, portfolios, journals
- Peer and self-assessments
- Self-reflections

CHAPTER 7 | Assessment and Inquiry Tools

Peer and Self-Assessment

Having students evaluate their own contributions during inquiry strengthens the learning experience and metacognition. This happens naturally throughout the process when the librarian or teacher checks in and asks, "How is it going for you? What is working, or not working, with your research?" Others times, a teacher may want a more formal method for students to evaluate themselves on a particular skill, such as defining their research questions, evaluating their types of sources, or mastering a particular writing style. Students who engage in self-evaluation are more likely to develop a feeling of empowerment and a sense of autonomy when they honestly look at their work and reflect on their efforts. When paired with clear targets and criteria, students can critically evaluate their own performance and internalize the criteria for judging success. The process can also generate new strategies that students can use to improve achievement. When done well, self-assessment results in greater motivation because it allows students to internalize new knowledge and skills.

Emily, a high school senior, was struggling with her focus when researching King Edward VIII of England, who abdicated the throne in order to marry an American socialite. She was finding only factual information during her research and wanted to approach the abdication from a different angle. Through conversations with her mentor group and her own self-reflection journal, she concluded that the interesting part of the story was not the abdication itself, but the qualities necessary to be a leader and how personal ambitions or personality strengths might assist or hinder one's ability to lead. Emily pivoted; she explored a new path of research and focused on the psychology of making choices, the qualities of effective leaders, and used King Edward as an example. The final presentation was well crafted and included multiple research studies from various disciplines that discussed leadership, personality traits, and risk taking. Emily reflected that she was glad she had switched her research, and she claims the original essay would have been dull. She also commented that she had taken time to reflect on her own personality to consider if she had the necessary traits to be a public leader. Would she risk everything if she traveled that path herself? This personal internalization of what Emily learned is the reason we want our students to think deeply and learn from others.

Inquiry Circle

When students have worked with an inquiry circle or mentor group, they are more willing to take risks and share their initial ideas, research probes, sources, or drafts with their peers. Peer evaluation can be very effective, but it also can be superficial. Students frequently evaluate each other's presentations and leave unfulfilling comments such as "good job" or "I like your images." As educators, we must create a culture of conversations, input, and thoughtful critique. We need to send the message that we "criticize/evaluate/discuss ideas—not people." Students who feel safe, and experience positive encounters with risk taking, will put more effort into peer evaluation—particularly if they feel the suggestions will make a difference and help their friends. Provide evaluation sentence starters or use an online discussion forum for input.

One way to establish an open culture of sharing and evaluation is to create multiple opportunities for inquiry circles to share their writing throughout the inquiry process. If students are willing to explain their reasoning behind the sources they chose for an annotated bibliography, then they may be open to analysis or critique of the types of sources they used. If students have the opportunity to read aloud their first drafts to a group, they may actually hear their own words and self-correct when the group members don't understand the meaning. If you want thoughtful commenting during the peer-review process, then you must allot time for the community to form and, most importantly, care.

Rubrics

Rubrics can be an effective means for providing peer-review prompts (see Table 7.2). Keep the language simple within the rubric, and ensure the statements are tied to learning targets. Provide ample time and multiple opportunities for students to evaluate one another's work. It is not necessary for everyone's work to be evaluated by every classmate because the quality of comments will diminish if students perceive the review to be too much work. Jump in and be an evaluator, too.

Table 7.2 Example of a Peer Reflection

Evaluator's Name:		Presentation by:	
Evaluate your classmate's presentation by being fair and accurate. Provide additional comments to justify your evaluation below.			
	Highly successful	Mostly successful	Needs Improvement
Content/Message The information was presented in a way that was easy to understand and organized in a logical manner.			
Interest/Engaging The presentation was interesting and made me want to listen. I learned new information from the presenter.			

	Highly successful	Mostly successful	Needs Improvement
Relevance/Application The presenter helped me to understand why I should care about this topic or motivated me to take action.			
Methodology The presentation method helped my understanding of the topic. Images, video/audio, or narration supported the learning goals and were not a distraction.			

Commendations: What aspects of the presentation were interesting, engaging, or made you care more about the topic?

Clarifying Questions: What information was missing or needs to be included so you understand the presentation better?

Extension Questions: What follow-up questions do you have for the presenter to help you dive deeper into the topic?

CHAPTER 7 | Assessment and Inquiry Tools

Other options for self- or peer-assessments include:

- Use an online discussion forum in a LMS for students to post ideas, and then have inquiry members give opinions in a public manner so all can learn from each other's comments.

- Modify the Socratic seminar methodology to discuss research questions and ask students to provide clarifying questions about each other's topics.

- Use a blog for an inquiry journal. Invite community members and experts to follow and comment to the students on their journey.

- Use video journals or simple recordings for students to discuss their work. Students might be willing to give additional feedback if the medium is simple and easy to use, like Flipgrid (www.flipgrid.com).

- Consider publishing student work in a classroom-created, peer-reviewed journal and have the evaluation comments from the reviewers be part of the introduction or appendix. This provides readers insight to the review process, and they can compare how the ideas or critiques improved the final version.

- Use an online form like the example in Table 7.3 to have students evaluate their own work habits and behaviors at the end of an inquiry project. Track these behaviors throughout the school year, and use reflections for personal goals.

Table 7.3 Personal Evaluation Form

LEARNING SKILLS AND WORK HABITS	1	2	3	4	5
Responsibility: Completes classwork and assignments according to timelines; manages own behavior; perseveres and makes an effort when responding to challenges.					
Independent Work: Independently monitors, assesses, and revises plans to complete tasks and meet goals; uses class time appropriately; follows instructions.					
Initiative: Acts on new ideas and opportunities for learning; willing to take risks; advocates for self and others.					
Organization: Creates and follows a plan for completing work and tasks; determines priorities and manages time to achieve goals; selects, evaluates, and uses information, technology, and resources to complete tasks.					
Collaboration: Responds positively to the ideas, opinions, and values of others; shares information, resources, and expertise, and promotes critical thinking to solve problems and make decisions.					
Reflection:					
Goals for next inquiry project:					

Summative Assessments

Summative assessments provide accountability, and they typically occur at the end of a learning activity to determine student understanding. They take on a broader perspective and are tied to learning standards for the curriculum. For example, a science assessment may determine whether students can generate or clarify questions, develop possible explanations, design and conduct investigations, and use data as evidence to support or reject their own explanations. An effective summative assessment closely mirrors the real work of the discipline.

Because the inquiry process lends itself naturally to formative assessments, the summative assessment should be used to make decisions about the quality of student learning on the basis of established learning targets. These criteria should be determined during the preplanning stages and presented from the very beginning so students are constantly working toward its goal. The summative assessment is customized depending on the final published format, and may be varied in format (rubric, culminating portfolio, performance task, oral presentation, written essay, capstone project), but it always assesses mastery and performance/production levels.

These four categories of knowledge and skills below are common to many subject areas and disciplines. Consider using these categories for summative assessments, and customize them for specific disciplines (Ontario Ministry of Education, 2010).

- ***Knowledge and understanding***: Subject-specific content acquired in each grade or course (knowledge), and the comprehension of its meaning and significance (understanding).
- ***Thinking***: The use of critical and creative thinking skills and/or processes.
- ***Communication***: The conveying of meaning through various forms.
- ***Application***: The use of knowledge and skills to make connections within and between various contexts.

Performance Tasks

Too many secondary students decide they are not proficient writers and struggle with developing an academic essay. Providing real-world application removes the pressure and stigma of low-level writers, who often have other qualities that make them inquisitive researchers. Consider having the summative assessment be a performance task instead of a written essay. If biology students observe animals in nature, have them design and make recommendations for a natural zoo habitat. Business students can create job descriptions and resumes for a student-run store. This style of assessment not only removes the temptation to plagiarize written work, but it closely mirrors performance reviews and projects in career fields.

The criteria for assessment of a performance task should focus on two areas: (1) understanding of the content and instructional goals; and (2) product and/or performance quality. Be careful because the student might do well on the performance task but have limited understanding of the content or be unable to connect what they've done to "big ideas" or instructional goals. Vice versa, students could do poorly on the performance assessment yet have a deep understanding of the material. Strike a balance between the two.

Librarian's Role

The librarian may be asked to be involved in the final summative assessment of the inquiry-based learning and to create a rubric for evaluation. For example, librarians could provide input on the diversity of sources, credibility of sources, quality of research, and/or citation format. The evaluation rubric could state whether the student was still in the beginning or developing stages, or if the student demonstrated proficient or excellent work. The librarian would need to be very involved throughout the inquiry process, and the students would need to document their process for this to be a credible and effective evaluation.

If the final summative assessment is a performance or presented to an authentic audience, the librarian can offer unique insights during the final evaluation. Whenever I am involved in performance task evaluation, I comment on student's use of credible sources, speak to their ability to push through difficult challenges, and offer insight on conclusions and summaries. Too often, the librarian is not included in assessment. I encourage you to insert yourself into the process and explain to the teacher the value you could add.

 In the Spotlight

Technology Assessment Tools

Dr. Paul Hampton uses Seesaw (web.seesaw.me/) to engage his high school science students while conducting inquiry-based lessons. Hampton asks students to make observations of a science phenomenon and describe what they see and know. Most educators view Seesaw as an elementary program, but Hampton uses it to check for understanding by having his high-school students diagram vocabulary words on their iPads, or document their learning so he can track everyone's comprehension at the same time. Students can take photos, sketch scientific processes, and add sources to their ongoing portfolio. Seesaw is the ultimate exit ticket because, as a teacher, you get immediate feedback whether students understood the lesson. Here are some other recommended formative or summative assessment tools.

Create interactive quizzes and presentations, and view real-time work of students:

> **Seesaw** (web.seesaw.me)
>
> **GoFormative** (goformative.com)
>
> **NearPod** (nearpod.com)

Use video or discussion forums for asynchronous conversation, peer review, and checks for understanding:

> **LMS: Canvas** (www.canvaslms.com), **Schoology** (www.schoology.com), or **Edmodo** (www.edmodo.com) all have built-in discussion forums.
>
> **Flipgrid** (info.flipgrid.com)

Use forms, surveys, or quiz software for student observations, self-evaluation, exit tickets, flash cards, student-response systems, or final assessments:

> **Google Forms** (docs.google.com/forms)
>
> **Quizlet** (quizlet.com)
>
> **Quizziz** (quizizz.com)
>
> **Socrative** (www.socrative.com)

Written work can be shared for peer review, commenting, or summative assessment using these tools:

> **Google Docs** (docs.google.com/document)
>
> **EduBlogs** (edublogs.org)
>
> **Kidblog** (kidblog.org/home)
>
> **Google Sites** (sites.google.com)

Use visual-thinking strategies to have students sketch out thinking, create visual notes for comprehension, or as a graphic organizer:

> **Paper by 53** (www.fiftythree.com)
>
> **Explain Everything** (explaineverything.com)
>
> **Notability** (gingerlabs.com)

Rubric creators assist teachers in creating assessments that are in kid-friendly language and tied to standards or learning targets:

> **RubiStar** (rubistar.4teachers.org/index.php)
>
> Most LMS programs (**Canvas, Schoology**) have rubric generators.

CHAPTER 8

Reflection for Deeper Learning

John Dewey's philosophy is that we do not learn from experience, we learn from reflecting on experience (Lash, 2018). Reflection can be a powerful experience for our secondary students during a time period when they are maturing and figuring out their own self-image as academic students. Tara Slaughter found reflection to be an absolutely vital component of the learning process for her own writing students: "The research process was impossible without daily or weekly reflection. I don't know how to be in touch with my students without their personal reflection." Slaughter used exit notes to communicate with her students, but she noticed that the students primarily discussed what they learned about themselves as researchers. Students commented on their own success or lack of progress, areas where they felt inadequate, and what they would do differently next time. "Reflection takes time because it's a muscle we don't use, and students need to build capacity to constructively critique their own work without tearing themselves down" (Personal communication). Slaughter's advice is to use inquiry circles to get students talking with each other about their challenges during research, but then have them individually reflect through exit tickets or student conferences.

Reflecting on Content and Process

Reflection of content can impact student's retention and learning. Even asking students to answer, "What was the central idea of your inquiry?" cements the material and helps with the transfer of big ideas to new concepts. If students had the opportunity to share their learning with an authentic audience, asking students if they felt the audience understood the purpose of their inquiry is a good indicator of comprehension. A reflection prompt that invites them to revisit the initial inquiry question and see if they feel satisfied with the answer might even lead students to further their knowledge with additional ideas for inquiry.

Our goal is to create students who are self-directed information seekers. Reflection on process helps students be aware of how they learned. Questions for a prompt might include: Do I need to talk to others to understand my ideas? Do I need quiet time to process information? Do I need time to think before I write down ideas? Does it help me to draw or organize my ideas visually? Do I need help getting started? These questions help students to understand themselves as learners without judgment or feelings of inadequacy as researchers.

Benefits of Reflection

There are many benefits of providing students opportunities to think critically about their own learning and habits. Regular and authentic reflection in a journal enables students to see the value of their own learning process. Too often, our students go through school and don't take the time to examine their experiences. The power of reflection can emphasize the significance of their accomplishments. Secondary students are self-aware and have a good idea of their own abilities. Students can identify where they did well, what didn't go as well as planned, and solutions for what they need to change. This growth mindset helps students to understand that learning is a process and a lifelong venture.

Regular reflection can also play a role with student advocacy. Carefully constructed conversations can provide students opportunities to design their own solutions and strategies to improve their learning. Since they propose the solutions, they are more likely to follow through versus acting on a teacher's suggestion of what they should do differently.

Reflection can also provide students with the motivation to learn and help them enjoy the learning process. I had a professor in my graduate program at Pepperdine University who called this "hard fun." We often struggled with challenging assignments that required deep thinking and collaboration to solve. Yet, when we reflected upon our successes (and failures), we understood that the struggle made the results even more precious. The motivation to continue comes from thinking about your own feelings and emotions, and understanding what drives your ambition.

Finally, memorizing content or listening to lectures does not help students become critical thinkers. Students shouldn't move through the curriculum without some type of real-world context or reflection. To deepen learning, students need to understand "why" they are researching important concepts and be able to answer, "So what?" Having the students work collaboratively to prepare inquiry charts with their answers fosters a sense of purpose. Critical thinking stems from pausing to truly understand the significance and impact of what they are learning.

Reflection Techniques

Reflection timelines can help students consider the stages of inquiry and the strategies they used to learn in each stage. Looking at each step of the inquiry process requires students to evaluate what worked or didn't work. Consider having students sketch a road map of their inquiry journey. Have students evaluate if specific inquiry tools were helpful (journals, inquiry circles, mentor groups, etc.). This teaches students more about their own learning styles and gives them ideas for what they would like to replicate in the next inquiry. The final reflection helps students to set goals for future inquiry projects; they share which aspects of the inquiry process was easy or hard for them and make plans for how they will tackle those situations in the future. Document these goals using digital portfolios so they can be easily reviewed before the next inquiry unit.

We want our students to build capacity beyond an inquiry unit or lesson. Meaningful questions will introduce new topics and interesting ideas for future exploration. The close of one unit opens a range of possible new ones. Do students have a place where they can document the new questions that arise from their research? A curiosity board or personal parking lot for research questions can stay with students from year to year. Many of the technology tools for assessment shared in Chapter 7 will work for reflection as well.

A final student–teacher or student–librarian reflection conference can be an effective tool, if time allows. Have students complete an individual inquiry assessment (survey, checklist, or brief written analysis) before attending so they come prepared to discuss their inquiry project. Conferencing provides a private forum for students who are less comfortable critiquing their own learning in a larger group. Teachers should focus on what the student reported in their reflection rather than the merits of the final product. This is also a great time to survey students to ask what the teacher could do to improve the inquiry process for them.

Reflection Questions

I have included a sampling of reflection questions (see Table 8.1) that can guide student thinking during the teacher conference or their own reflection. These questions can be used to provide one-on-one feedback for students or for peer review. They can be used in a blogging setting or with digital portfolios and are useful for class discussion or online bulletin boards. They can even be used to understand and inform which teaching strategies and activities were successful in the inquiry-based lesson. Review the full list of 40 reflection questions from Edutopia (2017).

CHAPTER 8 | Reflection for Deeper Learning

Table 8.1 Sampling of Reflection Questions *(Edutopia, 2017)*

Example questions for **looking back** on the learning process:	• What process did you go through to produce this piece? • What problems did you encounter? • How did you solve them?
Questions to ask that focus on **inward-looking**:	• How do you feel about this piece of work? • Did you meet your standards? • What did you learn about yourself as you worked on this piece?
Outward-looking reflection questions:	• Did you do your work the way other people did theirs? • Anything similar or different? • What is the one thing you particularly want people to notice when they look at your work?
Questions to focus on **forward-looking**:	• One thing I would like to improve upon is … • What's one goal you would like to set for yourself for next time? • What might you want next year's teacher to know about you (the things you are good at)?

Librarian Involvement with Reflection

As an educator who works with a wide variety of classroom teachers and grade levels, the librarian can offer a unique perspective across disciplines. Librarians can offer reflection ideas, common language, and strategies from other subject areas. I often find myself sharing a strategy that worked in the social studies department with the teachers in the world languages department. Sharing digital examples of how other teachers have used online discussion forums, video reflections, and peer reviews allows teachers to see the value of the reflection process and inspires them to try it in their own classes. I am there to coach them through the process or troubleshoot any technology issues.

Schedule multiple student reflection periods and understand its power. Because of the flexible nature of their position, the librarian can act as another interested adult in a student's learning process by asking them how it is going, if they are frustrated, and what they have learned from their research. Because the two teachers collaborated together on the unit plan, the librarian can inform the teacher of successes and pitfalls that occurred during the unit. Having critical checkpoints throughout the inquiry-based process means that adjustments can be made to ensure success for everyone. Reflection is an underused strategy, but one that can have the greatest impact.

Reflective Practices for the Inquiry Teachers

While it is important for students to reflect on their own learning, the teacher and librarian should also commit time to reflect on their planning, teaching strategies, and inquiry activities. By building in reflection time professionally, the educators can ask themselves, "If we were going to do it again, what would we change?" Discussions focus on what went well and identify difficulties the students experienced. The teacher and librarian can look at students who did not make sufficient progress, who did not dig deep enough into content, or who were unable to articulate their learning. What could be done differently? Together they can design an action plan that addresses instructional strategies that will impact the learning environment or evaluate the use of inquiry tools. The goal is to gain a new perspective on the past inquiry learning experience that they can apply to the next one. How powerful would it be for the teacher and librarian to share their own reflections about the inquiry process with their students, and model the value of learning and constantly trying to improve!

In the Spotlight

Self-Reflection Template

The Buck Institute for Education shares the Self-Reflection on Project Work template for educators to use. Wouldn't it be powerful if this reflection were used repeatedly over a period of several years? I think students would come to an understanding of their own personal learning style, while also showing their growth as researchers. Learners who see themselves as being in charge of their own learning take more responsibility than those who perceive their teachers as being in charge of their growth. Librarians are in a position to influence the school's curriculum policies and encourage the use of reflective practices such as digital portfolios or ongoing research journals or logs. Table 8.2 could be printed, converted to a form, or used in connection with several of the technology tools for assessment shared in Chapter 7.

Table 8.2 Self-Reflection on Project Work

SELF-REFLECTION ON PROJECT WORK
Think about what you did in this project, and how well the project went. Write your comments in the right column.
Student Name:
Project Name:
Driving Question:
List the major steps of the project:
About Yourself
What is the most important thing you learned in this project:
What do you wish you had spent more time on or done differently:
What part of the project did you do your best work on:
About the Project
What was the most enjoyable part of this project:
What was the least enjoyable part of this project:
How could your teacher(s) change this project to make it better next time:

Source: © 2011 Buck Institute for Education, used with permission.

CHAPTER 9

Librarian's Call to Action

Inquiry-based learning is a dynamic instructional strategy that leverages the power of curiosity. The varied dimensions of this strategy take intentional planning and dedication to do it right, but you witness seeds of curiosity bloom into something meaningful and real. Don't underestimate the power of student agency and reflection. Make authentic and empowering lessons your primary goal as an educator.

Get Started on Your Journey!

I want to encourage librarians to be more involved with inquiry-based learning. Do not allow yourself to be relegated to the beginning of a research project; you have so much to offer and can be of value to students and teachers. Pick one or two areas and make that your focus this school year. Following are 10 ideas to get you started on your inquiry-based learning journey.

1. Build Relationships

Find out what your teachers need to be successful with inquiry-based learning. Listen and consider their challenges. Admit when you don't have the answers, but say, "Let's figure this out together." Constantly ask, "How can I help, and how can we improve the student experience?" Understand that it takes time to build levels of trust, so plant ideas, nurture growth, and be positive. The reward will be teamwork that creates energy and excitement for everyone. What steps will you take this school year to build relationships with teachers in your school?

2. Set a Goal

Identify concrete areas where you want to make an impact. It will be easier to stay motivated and track your progress if you make your goals actionable and focused. SMART goals are defined as specific, measurable, achievable, results-focused, and time-bound. Start small. Establish a baseline of your reality, so you can aim for progress you can actually achieve. Consider trying an inquiry circle, planning a creative opener, or building in more time for reflection. Schedule your calendar with check-ins to track your progress. How can you identify a SMART goal that will have the greatest impact on your ability to incorporate inquiry-based learning?

3. Show Leadership

Become the inquiry expert at your school. Read the books in the recommended reading section of this book. Attend workshops and online webinars to improve your own knowledge. Communicate the value of inquiry to educational stakeholders in your district. Give presentations to the staff on creative-inquiry openers, online database resources, media literacy, or publishing options. Don't sit back and wait for the invitation to collaborate—join inquiry projects and bring your resource toolkit along. How will you make your passion visible?

4. Curate Resources

Purchase books and online resources to support inquiry-based projects in your school. Consider offering "mini-grants" to teachers who want to collaborate with you, and financially support their programs. Review your print and digital collection and make sure it matches your curriculum. Search online for experts, websites, videos, and community resources. Word will get out that you helped locate helpful resources and others will want in! Which project or curriculum area is ripe for revision and curation?

5. Address Excuses

Overcome barriers and the "Yeah, but ..." or "We've always done it this way" mentality head on. Focus on impacting student learning. Many are hesitant to try new instructional strategies because they fear failure. Too often, educators feel like they have to be perfect at everything before starting. Aim for (or at least expect) failure, and eventually it will happen less and less. Think of yourself as a positive and supportive inquiry coach. Gently push others to adopt a growth mindset. George Couros, author of *The Innovator's Mindset* (2015), says that to move an innovation culture forward, we need to help take people from *their* point A to *their* point B. We need to think about individuals and where they would like to move forward—and empower them to take a leap and go on that journey. How can you inspire innovation at your school?

6. Transform Your Library Space
Showcase inquiry projects in your library. Rotate student-created projects every month and invite community members to view the work. Hang motivational posters celebrating the inquiry process. Use your library space to shine a light on innovative projects. Schedule your library for expert presentations, project celebrations, and creative inquiry book displays. Consider your library space—does it scream collaboration and teamwork? If not, move the furniture to create workstations, a makerspace, or a publishing center. What changes need to happen in your library space to inspire curiosity and inquiry-based learning?

7. Build a Support Network
Surround yourself with like-minded people who are passionate about inquiry and research. Welcome involvement from other librarians in your district, passionate educators, and online communities. Consider reading this book together with a book group and use the discussion questions posed in each chapter. Support each other as you try out new ideas. How can you reach other educators who can support you in your efforts to be more involved in inquiry-based learning?

8. Grow a Personal Learning Network (PLN)
Create a PLN using social media. Many passionate educators share inquiry projects and resources on Twitter and other social media tools. Use the following hashtags to identify those tweets:

#inquiry	#passiondriven
#inquiryed	#designthinking
#inquiryk12	#tlchat (teacher-librarians)
#geniushour	#istelibs
#pbl	#FutureReadyLibs
#pblchat	

How can developing a PLN help you access and share resources?

9. Celebrate Your Success

Keep a list of your successes and review them when you feel defeated. Remember, FAIL means First Attempt In Learning. Not every inquiry project is going to be excellent, but when it is—share your success with your administrative staff, and share compliments about your collaborators. Make praise and recognition part of your school culture by sharing "rave reviews" or "applause" certificates of recognition at faculty meetings. The more other teachers hear about your successes, the more they will want to collaborate. How can you market your message of success and collaboration with your school community?

10. Teach Others

Share what you have learned about inquiry-based learning with other interested educators. Branch out and start a blog, share what is happening in your school. Let the local community know about what your students are doing. Present inquiry workshops to your district or community and bring your students along, if possible. Publish a journal article or write a book. Believe me, conducting interviews with inspiring librarians and researching examples of inquiry learning will change your own program. How can you be a leader in sharing the value of inquiry-based learning?

References

American Association of School Librarians. (2018). *National school library standards for learners, school librarians, and school libraries.* Chicago; ALA Editions.

American Library Association. (2017, August). *Teen literacies toolkit.* Retrieved from www.ala.org/yalsa/sites/ala.org.yalsa/files/content/TeenLiteraciesToolkit_WEB.pdf

AVID weekly: Teacher preparation. (2017). Retrieved from www.avidweekly.org/avid-teacher-preparation.html

Ballenger, B. (2012). *The curious researcher: a guide to writing research papers* (7th ed.). Boston, MA: Pearson Education, Inc.

Banchi, H., & Bell, R. (2008, October). The many levels of inquiry. *National Science Teachers Association*, 26–29. Retrieved from static.nsta.org/files/sc0810_26.pdf

Bergson-Michelson, T. (2017, September 6). *Imagine your perfect source: Strategies for cultivating expert researchers* [Webinar]. Retrieved from home.edweb.net/webinar/imagine-perfect-source-cultivating-expert-researchers/

Boss, S. (2013, October 28). *Are school librarians part of your PBL dream team?* [Web log post]. Retrieved from www.edutopia.org/blog/school-librarians-part-pbl-team-dream-suzie-boss

Boss, S. (2017, January 12). *Turning the community into a classroom* [Web log post]. Retrieved from www.edutopia.org/blog/turning-community-into-classroom-suzie-boss

Burvall, A. & Ryder, D. (2017). *Intention: Critical creativity in the classroom.* Irvine, CA: EdTechTeam Press.

Couros, G. (2015). *Innovator's mindset: Empower learning, unleash talent, and lead a culture of creativity.* San Diego, CA: Dave Burgess Consulting, Inc.

References

d.School. (2017). *K–12 lab network.* Retrieved from dschool.stanford.edu/programs/k12-lab-network

Daunic, R. (2017, September 22). *Four ways to integrate media literacy in the classroom.* Retrieved from www.commonsense.org/education/blog/4-ways-to-integrate-media-literacy-in-the-classroom

Donham, J. (2014). College ready—what can we learn from first-year college assignments? An examination of assignments in Iowa colleges and universities. *School Library Research, 17.* Retrieved from www.ala.org/aasl/sites/ala.org.aasl/files/content/aaslpubsandjournals/slr/vol17/SLR_CollegeReady_V17.pdf

E.L. Achieve. (2016). *About constructing meaning.* Retrieved from www.elachieve.org/what-we-do/about-constructing-meaning.html

California State University. (2010). *Evaluating information: Applying the CRAAP test.* [PDF file]. Retrieved from www.csuchico.edu/lins/handouts/eval_websites.pdf

Common Core State Standards Initiative. (2017). English language arts standards. Retrieved from www.corestandards.org/ELA-Literacy/

Evans, S. (2017, February 4). Krystyna's connection reflection. Retrieved from librarymediatechtalk.blogspot.com/2017/02/krystynas-connection-reflection.html

Ferriter, W. (2015, March 21). *What kind of school have you created?* [Web log post]. Retrieved from blog.williamferriter.com/2015/03/21/what-kind-of-school-have-you-created/

Forty reflection questions. (2017). Retrieved from backend.edutopia.org/sites/default/files/pdfs/stw/edutopia-stw-replicatingPBL-21stCAcad-reflection-questions.pdf

Future Ready Librarians. (2017). Unleashing the instructional leadership of librarians to foster future ready schools. Retrieved from futureready.org/program-overview/librarians/

Graves, C. (2016, June 7). Invention literacy research – part one. Retrieved from colleengraves.org/2016/06/07/invention-literacy-research-part-one

Guide to collaborative culture and shared leadership. (2001). *The Center for Collaborative Education*, 3-4. Retrieved from cce.org/files/Collaborative-Culture-and-Shared-Leadership.pdf

Harvard Project Zero. (2017). Visible thinking. Retrieved from www.visiblethinkingpz.org/VisibleThinking_html_files/VisibleThinking1.html

International Society for Technology in Education. (2016). ISTE standards for students. Retrieved from www.iste.org/standards/standards/for-students

Juliani, A. J. (2017a). *How to build a true culture of innovation at your school this year*. Retrieved from ajjuliani.com/culture-innovation/

Juliani, A. J. (2017b). *The research behind genius hour and choice in the classroom*. Retrieved from ajjuliani.com/research/

Juliani, A. J. (2017c). *Inquiry and innovation in the classroom: Using 20% time, genius hour, and PBL to drive student success*. New York, NY: Routledge.

Kuhlthau, C. C., Maniotes, L. K., & Caspari, A. K. (2012). *Guided inquiry design: A framework for inquiry in your school*. Santa Barbara, CA: ABC-CLIO.

Larmer, J. (2015, July 13). *Project-based learning vs. problem-based learning vs. X-BL* [Web log post]. Retrieved from www.edutopia.org/blog/pbl-vs-pbl-vs-xbl-john-larmer

Larmer, J., Mergendoller, J., & Boss, S. (2015). *Setting the standard for project based learning: A proven approach to Rigorous Classroom Instruction*. Alexandria, VA: ASCD.

Lash, J. (2018). When Students Stop and Think About What They're Learning. *Education Digest, 83*(6), 9.

References

Luhtala, M. (2017, January 18). *Personalizing instruction through the library* [Webinar]. Retrieved from home.edweb.net/webinar/personalizing-instruction-through-the-library/

Mackenzie, T. (2016). *Dive into inquiry*. Irvine, CA: EdTech Team Press.

Catlin Gabel School. (2017). Make your place. Retrieved from www.catlin.edu/page.cfm?p=1560

Maniotes, L. K., Harrington, L. & Lambusta, P. (Eds.). (2017). *Guided inquiry design in action: High school*. Santa Barbara, CA: ABC-CLIO.

Musallam, R. (2017). *Spark learning: 3 keys to embracing the power of student curiosity*. San Diego, CA: Dave Burgess Consulting, Inc.

Meyer, D. (2011, May 11). *The three acts of a mathematical story* [Web log post]. Retrieved from blog.mrmeyer.com/2011/the-three-acts-of-a-mathematical-story/

Michaelson, E. (2014, March 5). *With "GeniusCon project," students connect and problem solve* [Web log post]. Retrieved from www.slj.com/2014/03/schools/with-geniuscon-project-students-connect-and-problem-solve/

National Association for Media Literacy Education. (2007, November). Core principles of media literacy education in the United States. Retrieved from namle.net/publications/core-principles

National Council for the Social Studies. (n.d.). *National curriculum standards for social studies: Chapter 2—the themes of social studies*. Retrieved from www.socialstudies.org/standards/strands

Navarre Cleary. (2012). *Top ten reasons students plagiarize and what you can do about it* [PDF file]. Retrieved from offices.depaul.edu/oaa/faculty-resources/teaching/academic-integrity/Documents/Top%20Ten%20Reasons%20Students%20Plagiarize%202012.pdf

News literacy project: The need. (2017). Retrieved from www.thenewsliteracyproject.org/about/need

NoodleTools. (2017). *Your full-service classroom environment for the research process.* Retrieved from www.noodletools.com/wp/wp-content/uploads/2015/09/executive_summary_k12.pdf

Ophea. (2016). *Inquiry-based learning in health and physical education: A resource guide for educators* [PDF file]. Toronto, Ontario. Retrieved from teachingtools.ophea.net/sites/default/files/pdf/ibl_guide.pdf

Ontario Ministry of Education. (2010). *Growing success: Assessment, evaluation and reporting in Ontario schools, covering grades 1 to 12* (1st ed.) [PDF file]. Retrieved from www.edu.gov.on.ca/eng/policyfunding/growSuccess.pdf

Purdue Writing Lab. (2017). *Avoiding plagiarism.* Retrieved from owl.english.purdue.edu/owl/resource/589/1/

Ray, M. (2016, November 21). *Why not unleash the instructional leadership of librarians to foster future ready schools?* [Web log post]. Retrieved from futureready.org/not-unleash-instructional-leadership-librarians-foster-future-ready-schools/

Robinson, K. (2009). *The element: How finding your passion changes everything.* New York: Penguin.

Rothstein, D., & Santana, L. (2011, September/October). *Make just one change: Teaching children to ask their own questions.* Retrieved from hepg.org/hel-home/issues/27_5/helarticle/teaching-students-to-ask-their-own-questions_507.

Salmons, J. (2017, January 31). *Creating a culture of inquiry in the classroom* [Web log post]. Retrieved from www.methodspace.com/creating-culture-inquiry-classroom/

Self-reflection on project work. (2011). Retrieved from www.bie.org/object/document/self_reflection_on_project_work

Shippee, M. (2015, October 8). *A match made in heaven: Google Maps and augmented reality* [Web log post]. Retrieved from micahshippee.wordpress.com/2015/10/08/a-match-made-in-heaven-google-maps-and-augmented-reality/

References

Valenza, J. (2016, November 26). *Truth, truthiness, triangulation: A news literacy toolkit for a "post-truth" world* [Web log post]. Retrieved from blogs.slj.com/neverendingsearch/2016/11/26/truth-truthiness-triangulation-and-the-librarian-way-a-news-literacy-toolkit-for-a-post-truth-world/

Valenza, J. (2017, October 29). *Some secret strategies for serious searchers* [Web log post]. Retrieved from blogs.slj.com/neverendingsearch/2017/10/29/some-secret-strategies-for-serious-searchers/

Wagner, T. (2012a, April). Calling all innovators. *Educational Leadership, 69*(7), 66–69.

Wagner, T. (2012b). *Creating innovators* [PowerPoint slides]. Retrieved from www.tonywagner.com/downloads/

Wagner, T. (2017). *Tony Wagner's seven survival skills.* Retrieved October 26, 2017, from www.tonywagner.com/7-survival-skills/

Wiggins, G. & McTighe, J. (2005). *Understanding by design* (2nd ed.). Alexandria, VA: ASCD.

Wiggins, G. & McTighe, J. (2011). *The understanding by design guide to creating high-quality units.* Alexandria, VA: ASCD.

Wineburg, S., McGrew, S., Breakstone, J. & Ortega, T. (2016). *Evaluating information: The cornerstone of civic online reasoning* [PDF file]. Retrieved from sheg.stanford.edu/upload/V3LessonPlans/Executive%20Summary%2011.21.16.pdf

APPENDIX A
ISTE Standards

ISTE Standards for Students

The ISTE Standards for Students emphasize the skills and qualities we want for students, enabling them to engage and thrive in a connected, digital world. The standards are designed for use by educators, across the curriculum, with every age student, with a goal of cultivating these skills throughout a student's academic career. Both students and teachers will be responsible for achieving foundational technology skills to fully apply the standards. The reward, however, will be educators who skillfully mentor and inspire students to be agents of their own learning and amplify that learning with technology

1. **Empowered Learner**
   Students leverage technology to take an active role in choosing, achieving and demonstrating competency in their learning goals, informed by the learning sciences. Students:

   a. articulate and set personal learning goals, develop strategies leveraging technology to achieve them and reflect on the learning process itself to improve learning outcomes.

   b. build networks and customize their learning environments in ways that support the learning process.

   c. use technology to seek feedback that informs and improves their practice and to demonstrate their learning in a variety of ways.

   d. understand the fundamental concepts of technology operations, demonstrate the ability to choose, use and troubleshoot current technologies and are able to transfer their knowledge to explore emerging technologies.

2. **Digital Citizen**
   Students recognize the rights, responsibilities and opportunities of living, learning and working in an interconnected digital world, and they act and model in ways that are safe, legal and ethical. Students:

   a. cultivate and manage their digital identity and reputation and are aware of the permanence of their actions in the digital world.

   b. engage in positive, safe, legal and ethical behavior when using technology, including social interactions online or when using networked devices.

   c. demonstrate an understanding of and respect for the rights and obligations of using and sharing intellectual property.

   d. manage their personal data to maintain digital privacy and security and are aware of data-collection technology used to track their navigation online.

3. **Knowledge Constructor**
   Students critically curate a variety of resources using digital tools to construct knowledge, produce creative artifacts and make meaningful learning experiences for themselves and others. Students:

   a. plan and employ effective research strategies to locate information and other resources for their intellectual or creative pursuits.

   b. evaluate the accuracy, perspective, credibility and relevance of information, media, data or other resources.

   c. curate information from digital resources using a variety of tools and methods to create collections of artifacts that demonstrate meaningful connections or conclusions.

   d. build knowledge by actively exploring real-world issues and problems, developing ideas and theories and pursuing answers and solutions.

4. Innovative Designer
Students use a variety of technologies within a design process to identify and solve problems by creating new, useful or imaginative solutions. Students:
   a. know and use a deliberate design process for generating ideas, testing theories, creating innovative artifacts or solving authentic problems.
   b. select and use digital tools to plan and manage a design process that considers design constraints and calculated risks.
   c. develop, test and refine prototypes as part of a cyclical design process.
   d. exhibit a tolerance for ambiguity, perseverance and the capacity to work with open-ended problems.

5. Computational Thinker
Students develop and employ strategies for understanding and solving problems in ways that leverage the power of technological methods to develop and test solutions. Students:
   a. formulate problem definitions suited for technology-assisted methods such as data analysis, abstract models and algorithmic thinking in exploring and finding solutions.
   b. collect data or identify relevant data sets, use digital tools to analyze them, and represent data in various ways to facilitate problem-solving and decision-making.
   c. break problems into component parts, extract key information, and develop descriptive models to understand complex systems or facilitate problem-solving.
   d. understand how automation works and use algorithmic thinking to develop a sequence of steps to create and test automated solutions.

6. **Creative Communicator**

    Students communicate clearly and express themselves creatively for a variety of purposes using the platforms, tools, styles, formats and digital media appropriate to their goals. Students:

    a. choose the appropriate platforms and tools for meeting the desired objectives of their creation or communication.

    b. create original works or responsibly repurpose or remix digital resources into new creations.

    c. communicate complex ideas clearly and effectively by creating or using a variety of digital objects such as visualizations, models or simulations.

    d. publish or present content that customizes the message and medium for their intended audiences.

7. **Global Collaborator**

    Students use digital tools to broaden their perspectives and enrich their learning by collaborating with others and working effectively in teams locally and globally. Students:

    a. use digital tools to connect with learners from a variety of backgrounds and cultures, engaging with them in ways that broaden mutual understanding and learning.

    b. use collaborative technologies to work with others, including peers, experts or community members, to examine issues and problems from multiple viewpoints.

    c. contribute constructively to project teams, assuming various roles and responsibilities to work effectively toward a common goal.

    d. explore local and global issues and use collaborative technologies to work with others to investigate solutions.

© 2016 International Society for Technology in Education. ISTE® is a registered trademark of the International Society for Technology in Education. If you would like to reproduce this material, please contact permissions@iste.org.

APPENDIX B

Recommended Reading

Inquiry

Kuhlthau, C. C., Maniotes, L. K., & Caspari, A. K. (2012). *Guided inquiry design: A framework for inquiry in your school*. Santa Barbara, CA: ABC-CLIO.

Curriculum Design

Wiggins, G., & McTighe, J. (2011). *The understanding by design guide to creating high-quality units*. Alexandria, VA: ASCD.

Media Literacy

Baker, F. W. (2012). *Media literacy in the K–12 classroom*. United States of America: International Society for Technology in Education.

Design Thinking

Spencer, J., & Juliani, A. J. (2016). *Launch: Using design thinking to boost creativity and bring out the maker in every student*. San Diego, CA: Dave Burgess Publishing, LLC.

Innovation

Couros, G. (2015). *Innovator's mindset: Empower learning, unleash talent, and lead a culture of creativity*. San Diego, CA: Dave Burgess Consulting, Inc.

APPENDIX C
Discussion Questions

Reading *Inspiring Curiosity: A Librarian's Guide to Inquiry-Based Learning* together with a personal learning community (PLC) can benefit all involved. Bring librarians and classroom teachers together to reflect on the practice of teaching research, inspiring curiosity, and empowering students to design and implement authentic inquiry-based learning. Use these chapter questions to guide your reading and discussion.

Chapter 1

1. Compare Kate's experience with choosing her topic for inquiry-based learning from Chapter 1 with a student in your class/library. How does the student's own inquiry questions propel their research forward?

2. As you read this book, make a list of key entry points where librarians can insert themselves into inquiry-based lessons. Review them later on and create a plan of action.

3. Read the quote by Tony Wagner in Chapter 1. Do you agree or disagree with Wagner's statement about the single most competitive advantage? Why or why not.

4. Is a culture of student empowerment and openness evident at your school? Give specific examples or share goals for achieving this.

Chapter 2

1. Share which of the following areas is your strength and which ones you need to work on to be an effective inquiry

leader: build relationships, be of value, show empathy, or get involved.

2. Not all inquiry-based learning needs to embrace open inquiry. How can you use confirmation, structured, guided, or open inquiry effectively in the classroom or library?

3. Backwards planning and collaboration with a classroom teacher is key to success when using inquiry-based learning. What is preventing this from happening in your school situation and what are steps you can take to remedy it?

4. Guided Inquiry Design is an excellent resource for librarians and inquiry-based learning. How is this model the same or different than other research models you have used?

Chapter 3

1. Pick three powerful openers from this list and explain how you would use them with inquiry-based learning:

   Video/Film

   Non-Fiction or Literature Novels

   Teen Writers

   Social Justice Issues/Service Learning

   News Resources

   Primary Sources

   Connecting with Experts

   Real World Science, Math & Health

   Arts & Culture

2. John Larmer, editor of BIE suggests that problem-based learning, design thinking, project-based learning, place-based learning, etc. are "modern versions" of the same

concept. Which discipline lends itself to their "distinct flavor"?

3. Multiple technology tools and resources for powerful openers were shared in Chapter 3. How do you as a librarian or classroom teacher stay up-to-date on the latest trends and resources in education? What are your "go to" strategies or tools?

Chapter 4

1. Watch this video of the Question Formulation Technique: www.youtube.com/watch?v=lfXEf0nG51I. How is this technique different than teacher-directed questioning at the beginning of a lesson?

2. Visible Thinking routines provide scaffolding so students can document what they are reading and processing. Review the routines at goo.gl/q92K3e (Review Core, Understanding, Fairness, Truth and Creative routines) and share one that you find useful.

3. Genius Hour and Mentor Groups are two instructional strategies that may be more effective with different age groups or disciplines. Which teachers at your school or subject areas might be open to these ideas? How can you assist them in being successful?

Chapter 5

1. How do you approach teaching secondary students how to search effectively? Does your school or district have a comprehensive search curriculum? How do you determine when and what to teach to various grade levels?

2. How do you curate and organize the resources you share with students or teachers. How is this communicated to

your staff? How do you teach students to curate their own resources?

3. In this day of "fake news" and unreliable sources, what can we do as librarians to combat plagiarism and encourage Media Literacy and the evaluation of sources?

4. Does your school or district have a designated note-taking system? How does the librarian support its use?

5. Share strategies and techniques you use to differentiate instruction, reading, and research for special populations (English Language Learners, Special Education, High Achievers, etc.)

Chapter 6

1. Look through the list of publishing options listed in Chapter 6. Find three ideas that spark your interest and describe how you would use it for a future project?

2. Who or what are untapped resources or audiences in your school community that could be contacted for curriculum projects (local organizations, community leaders, parents, etc.). How can their involvement enrich the inquiry-based projects of secondary students?

Chapter 7

1. Inquiry tools can add concrete structure to your inquiry-based lessons. How could you use Inquiry Tools: Circles, Journals, Logs, and Charts with your school community? Is one more effective than others?

2. Inquiry-based learning offers multiple opportunities for both formative and summative assessments. How can you as the librarian be more involved in this area?

APPENDIX C | Discussion Questions

Chapter 8

1. Reflection is often overlook as an important aspect of inquiry-based learning. Just reading this book is asking you to reflect on your experience as a librarian or classroom teacher. How can reflection benefit you or your students?

2. As an educator who works with a variety of teachers, share how a technique that is used in one department could be also used in another department. How are instructional strategies shared among teachers at your school or district?

Chapter 9

1. Read through the Librarian's Call to Action in Chapter 9. Pick one or two areas and make that your focus this school year. Share and write down three specific steps that will make this happen this school year.